T0299999

'This is an excellent and thought-provoking book on the epistemology of testimony, one that deserves to be read by all who work in this field.'

Duncan Pritchard, *University of California, Irvine, USA;*
University of Edinburgh, UK

'Stephen Wright's book offers a thorough defence of the view that testimony functions to transmit knowledge and justification. In doing so it casts new light on familiar debates, and should be regarded as essential reading for anyone working in the epistemology of testimony.'

Paul Faulkner, *University of Sheffield, UK*

'Wright's excellent book presents a detailed defense of the idea that testimony transmits epistemic grounds from speaker to audience, and uses this idea to assess various other familiar accounts of testimony. It addresses all of the major issues in the epistemology of testimony and will be required reading for anyone interested in the topic.'

Sanford Goldberg, *Northwestern University, USA*

Knowledge Transmission

Our knowledge of the world comes from various sources. But it is sometimes said that testimony, unlike other sources, transmits knowledge from one person to another.

In this book, Stephen Wright investigates what the transmission of knowledge involves and the role that it should play in our theorising about testimony as a source of knowledge. He argues that the transmission of knowledge should be understood in terms of the more fundamental concept of the transmission of epistemic grounds, and that the claim that testimony transmits knowledge is not only defensible in its own right but also indispensable to an adequate theory of testimony. This makes testimony unlike other epistemic sources.

Stephen Wright is Lecturer in Philosophy at University College, Oxford, UK. With Sanford Goldberg, he is editor of *Memory and Testimony: New Philosophical Essays* (forthcoming).

Routledge Focus on Philosophy

Routledge Focus on Philosophy is an exciting and innovative new series, capturing and disseminating some of the best and most exciting new research in philosophy in short book form. Peer reviewed and, at a maximum of fifty thousand words, shorter than the typical research monograph, *Routledge Focus on Philosophy* titles are available in both ebook and print on demand format. Tackling big topics in a digestible format, the series opens up important philosophical research for a wider audience, and as such is invaluable reading for the scholar, researcher and student seeking to keep their finger on the pulse of the discipline. The series also reflects the growing interdisciplinarity within philosophy and will be of interest to those in related disciplines across the humanities and social sciences.

Available:

The Passing of Temporal Well-Being
Ben Bramble

How We Understand Others
Shannon Spaulding

Political Theory and Global Climate Action
Idil Boran

Consciousness and Moral Status
Joshua Shepherd

Knowledge Transmission
Stephen Wright

For more information about this series, please visit: www.routledge.com/Routledge-Focus-on-Philosophy/book-series/RFP

Knowledge Transmission

Stephen Wright

LONDON AND NEW YORK

First published 2019
by Routledge
2 Park Square, Milton Park, Abingdon, Oxon OX14 4RN

and by Routledge
605 Third Avenue, New York, NY 10017

First issued in paperback 2020

Routledge is an imprint of the Taylor & Francis Group, an informa business

British Library Cataloguing-in-Publication Data
A catalogue record for this book is available from the British Library

Library of Congress Cataloging-in-Publication Data
Names: Wright, Stephen (Stephen John), author.
Title: Knowledge transmission / Stephen Wright.
Description: 1 [edition]. | New York : Routledge, 2018. | Series:
   Routledge focus on philosophy | Includes bibliographical
   references and index.
Identifiers: LCCN 2018023124 | ISBN 9781138085275
   (hardback : alk. paper) | ISBN 9781315111384 (e-book)
Subjects: LCSH: Knowledge, Theory of. | Testimony.
Classification: LCC BD181 .W75 2018 | DDC 121—dc23
LC record available at https://lccn.loc.gov/2018023124

ISBN 13: 978-0-367-73368-1 (pbk)
ISBN 13: 978-1-138-08527-5 (hbk)

Typeset in Times New Roman
by Apex CoVantage, LLC

To my parents

Contents

Preface

At the outset of *How to Do Things With Words*, J.L. Austin says the following:

> What I have to say here is neither difficult nor contentious; the only merit I should like to claim for it is that of being true, at least in parts.

I'm never quite sure whether this is bombastic or modest from Austin. On the one hand, claiming to have arrived at the truth in philosophy – even in a limited way – is liable to be contentious. On the other, Austin explicitly disavows saying anything radical or groundbreaking. In any event, I should like to claim the opposite on behalf of this book. I think that what I have to say in this discussion *is* difficult and contentious, at least in parts. At any rate, it's taken me a lot of time and effort to come up with it. As for whether or not it's true, I'll leave that for the reader to decide.

Allow me to begin by recommending two very good books on the epistemology of testimony (neither of which is this one). The first is *Learning from Words*, by Jennifer Lackey. The second is *Knowledge on Trust*, by Paul Faulkner. My thinking on the epistemology of testimony and the transmission of knowledge began just before I started my doctoral work. I read *Learning from Words* and found it fascinating. I think that, at the time, I agreed with just about every claim in the book. And when *Knowledge on Trust* came out, I agreed with everything in that, too.

Two things should become clear in the following discussion. The first is that I've subsequently found substantial amounts to disagree with in each case. The second is that, my dissent notwithstanding, *Learning from Words* and *Knowledge on Trust* are the works that have influenced my thinking more than any others. I owe an enormous intellectual debt to the authors of each. *Learning from Words* paved the way for me to think clearly about the epistemology of testimony and *Knowledge on Trust* provided the stimulus for discussing the idea of knowledge transmission in the way that I do in this book.

The internal structure of the book is as follows: Chapters 1, 2 and 3 consider the question of what the transmission of knowledge involves and the conditions under which it takes place. I argue that the transmission of knowledge is grounded in a more fundamental notion of the transmission of epistemic grounds, that a speaker's testimony transmitting knowledge depends on her saying what she does because she knows it and that a listener acquiring knowledge through transmission does *not* depend on her being aware of reasons for believing what the speaker says.

In Chapters 4, 5 and 6, I argue for the indispensability of transmission to a complete epistemology of testimony. This is done first by arguing that competing *internalist* and *reliabilist* approaches to the epistemology of testimony are unable to give a complete account of how testimony functions as a source of knowledge. With this in hand, I argue that an approach that endorses knowledge transmission *can* give achieve completeness in this regard.

Lastly, in Chapter 7, I argue for the defensibility of a transmission theory of testimony. Transmission theories have come under fire from various objections in the recent epistemology of testimony. Those objections purport to show that the concept of transmission is either false, incoherent or otherwise dispensable to the epistemology of testimony. I argue that these objections are inconclusive against the transmission theory of testimony I develop.

I have always thought that testimony transmits knowledge. And the result of that, after various processes of refinement, is this book. During my doctoral years, I had a lot of help trying to work out what I meant by transmission and why it should be of any use to anyone in thinking about the epistemology of testimony. Paul Faulkner showed me why all of the reasons I initially had for endorsing transmission were terrible and helped me to see why, the impotence of those reasons notwithstanding, the idea of transmission might be worth thinking about. Miranda Fricker and Rob Hopkins also provided invaluable help in figuring out how to get the ideas that I wanted to develop straight and how to avoid running into philosophical pitfalls. I'm fearful that they might not have managed to save me from all of them.

I've subsequently been fortunate enough to have had valuable and useful conversations with various people. These have made the present work exponentially better than it would otherwise have been. Duncan Pritchard and Eric Olson examined my doctoral thesis on the issues that I discuss here and the discussion at the *viva* proved extremely valuable in working out how to get things across and how to refine the views that I had. Lucy Campbell, Rachel Fraser, Sandy Goldberg, Katherine Hawley, Arnon Keren, Guy Longworth, Robin McKenna and Martin Pickup all deserve special mentions for the help they've given me in thinking about or talking through issues with me. I'd like to say individually how each of them has helped, but there isn't space.

Material from this discussion has been presented at conferences and workshops in Barcelona, Bologna, Cambridge, Cardiff, Copenhagen, Edinburgh, Glasgow, Hull, Kent, Leeds, Madrid, Nottingham, Oxford, Paris, Sheffield, Stirling, Stockholm, Vienna and Warwick. A lot of audiences have had to listen to a lot of material in one form or another and I'm grateful to everyone who has done so. I'm also grateful to Tony Bruce and Adam Johnson at Routledge and Hattie Pickup and Nicole Woodford for proofreading.

I'm also grateful to colleagues who have supported my development, both in Oxford and in Sheffield. Since I arrived in Oxford, I've worked at various colleges, and I've been fortunate to have had wonderfully supportive colleagues throughout my time here. So I'm grateful to Bill Child, Anil Gomes and Andreas Mogensen. In particular, I'm grateful to Geoffrey Ferrari and Alex Lumbers, who offered me my first academic job, as I was finishing up in Sheffield. I must have represented something of an unproven entity and I'm grateful to them for giving me an opportunity.

Of course, I'm grateful to my parents, to whom this work is dedicated, for a lifetime of support. And last of all, I'm grateful to Ona, who has encouraged me in this project from its proposal to its eventual completion.

1 What is transmission?

What is it to know that ϕ? As my first-year undergraduates tell me, this is a vexed question, the discussion of which has already taken up several books. Here are four ideas about knowledge:

(1) To know that ϕ is to form one's belief that ϕ on the basis of a reason for ϕ that one is aware of.

(2) To know that ϕ is to form one's belief that ϕ through a process that has certain properties.

(3) To know that ϕ is to be in a mental state that entails ϕ.

(4) To know that ϕ is to have the ability to be guided by the fact that ϕ.

Each of these ideas can be developed in various ways.

When developing **(1)**, one might ask what kind of reasons are sufficient to underpin knowledge that ϕ. Various answers may be given. One is that only reasons that guarantee the truth of ϕ can ground knowledge that ϕ.[1] A second allows that reasons can ground knowledge that ϕ even if they do not guarantee the truth of ϕ.[2] A third answer suggests that the strength of reasons required for knowledge that ϕ can vary according to the particular details of the case.[3]

When considering **(2)**, one might ask what properties the process in question must have. Again, various answers are available. One answer is that the subject's belief must be caused by the fact that ϕ.[4] A second answer is that the process must be *reliable*, in that it generally yields true, rather than false, beliefs in close possible worlds.[5] A third answer is that the process must be *safe*, which means that it would not easily yield a false belief with respect to ϕ.[6] A fourth answer is that the process must be *sensitive* in that, if ϕ were false, then it would not yield the belief that ϕ, and if ϕ were true, then it would yield the belief that ϕ.[7]

Instead of taking either of these views, one might hold the view that knowing that ϕ is a matter of being in a mental state that entails ϕ. This is the view given in **(3)**.[8] When one sees that ϕ, hears that ϕ or remembers that ϕ, one comes to know that ϕ. The mental state associated with seeing, hearing or remembering that ϕ is factive. That is to say, one cannot see, hear or remember that ϕ unless ϕ is the case. Furthermore, to know that ϕ is just to be in one or another of these mental states, or some other mental state that guarantees the truth of ϕ.

The view in **(4)** is the least prominent.[9] According to this view, when one knows that ϕ one is in a position to use the fact that ϕ, as opposed to merely the proposition that ϕ or the fact that one believes that ϕ, when deliberating or deciding how to act. However, the idea of knowledge as an ability is not merely that someone who knows that ϕ is in a position to be guided by the fact that ϕ. Instead, the idea is that knowing that ϕ just is a matter of having this ability. Rather than thinking of knowing that ϕ as being in a particular state that allows one to be guided by the fact that ϕ, the view expressed in **(2)** is that knowledge that ϕ is nothing other than the ability to be guided by the fact that ϕ.

There is thus substantial disagreement about what knowledge amounts to. There is also substantial disagreement over exactly what is involved in giving an account of knowledge. Those who endorse either **(1)** or **(2)** typically think that giving an account of knowledge involves giving an account of which beliefs amount to knowledge. Those who endorse **(3)** or **(4)**, by contrast, do not. Endorsing **(3)** involves taking knowledge as the starting point for the elucidation of epistemological concepts and using it to give accounts of other notions, such as belief. Endorsing **(4)**, on the other hand, changes the project of giving an account of knowledge into the project of giving an account of how an ability is manifested.

For my own part, I have a lot of sympathy with the idea of knowledge as an ability, as expressed in **(4)**, but I mean for the discussion here to be neutral between any of these approaches to knowledge. This involves finding some sort of usable common ground between them. Fortunately, this can be done. Each approach takes knowledge to be a relation between a knowing subject and a propositional object which, for the purpose of this discussion, I shall call a fact. Of course, one might reject the idea that the objects of knowledge are facts and opt for an account of knowledge according to which the objects of knowledge are true propositions (where true propositions are distinct from facts). In such a case, the ideas that I shall put forward can be reinterpreted in the language of true propositions. For ease of expression, I shall refer to the objects of knowledge as facts.

Consider a straightforward case in which someone sees what she recognises as a church in front of her. The lighting is good, her visual processes function normally and there is no misleading evidence that would cause her to doubt that there is a church in front of her. The subject in this situation is in a position to know that there is a church in front of her. Whether this is because she is aware of reasons for thinking that the thing in front of her is a church, because of some fact about her visual processes, because she has the ability to be guided by the fact that there is a church in front of her or because she is in a mental state that entails that there is a church in front of her, the subject is in a position to know that there is a church in front of her – she is related to the fact that there is a church in front of her in a particular way.

Not all knowledge comes about in this way, though. We know many things that we have not seen – that the Battle of Agincourt took place in the year 1415, that cobalt has the atomic number 27 and that Uranus has (at least) 27 moons. This information comes to us through the testimony of others. The fact that we have not seen these things for ourselves does not undermine the idea that we have knowledge of these facts. It seems that taking the testimony of others can therefore be a perfectly respectable way of coming to know things.[10] If this is correct, then it seems that testimony can, in the right circumstances, bring about the same kind of relation between a subject and a fact that is brought about when the subject sees something.

This is not to say that testimony can bring us to see something. This is an idea that Locke (1689) rightly poured scorn on. Rather, it is to say that seeing that ϕ and being told that ϕ can both put someone in a position to know that ϕ. Although Locke poured scorn on the idea that testimony allows us to see with someone else's eyes, it is altogether more plausible that he left open the idea that being told that ϕ might put someone in a position to know that ϕ.[11]

These observations prompt the question of how testimony facilitates the relationship between a subject and a fact. In other words, the question concerns how being told something puts a listener in a position to know the truth of what the speaker says. At this early stage, however, we should distinguish between the question of *how* testimony puts a listener in a position to know the truth of what a speaker says and the question of *under what conditions* testimony puts a listener in a position to know the truth of what a speaker says.

In his discussion of the nature of knowledge, John Hyman (2015) urges us to distinguish between the question of what knowledge is and the question of how, if at all, knowledge of various kinds is possible. In Hyman's words, 'the point I should like to emphasise is that the question of what knowledge is and the question of how it is acquired are quite different, even though they are connected' (Hyman 2015, p. 160). Likewise, in the discussion here, the question of how testimony puts a listener in a position to know the truth of what a speaker says and the question of under what conditions the speaker's testimony puts a listener in a position to know the truth of what a speaker says will be kept apart and considered in turn.

An example helps to illustrate the difference between the two. Consider the example of iron rusting. An account of how iron rusts might appeal to the process of losing oxygen atoms, or the oxygen combining with the iron at an atomic level. An account of the conditions under which iron rusts might appeal to the presence of oxygen, iron and moisture. This is not to say that the two questions are independent of one another. Knowing the answer to one might put someone in a position to infer the answer to the other. Nevertheless, they are conceptually different.

How, then, does testimony that φ put a listener in a position to know that φ? One candidate answer is that knowledge from testimony is fundamentally similar to knowledge from instruments. In the same way that the reading on the thermometer puts an observer in a position to know that the ambient temperature is 26°C, a speaker's testimony that φ puts a listener in a position to know that φ. This basic idea can be understood in different ways.

One idea is that a thermometer puts an observer in a position to know that the ambient temperature is 26°C because the observer is aware of various reasons for thinking that the thermometer's reading is an accurate indicator of the ambient temperature. The observer can thus form her belief on the basis of these reasons and thereby come to be related to the fact that the ambient temperature is 26°C such that she knows it. In the same way, when a speaker tells a listener that φ, her testimony puts the listener in a position to know that φ because the listener is aware of various reasons for thinking that the speaker's testimony that φ is a good indication that φ. Believing on the basis of these reasons allows the listener to know that φ.

This is the basic idea behind *internalist* approaches to the epistemology of testimony. These approaches will be the subject of Chapter 4. But the idea that knowledge from testimony is fundamentally similar to knowledge from instruments is not unique to internalist approaches. Another way of thinking about the epistemology of instruments involves taking it that the thermometer's deliverance puts an observer in a position to know that the ambient temperature is 26°C simply because it is a reliable indication of this, regardless of whether or not the observer is aware of any reasons for thinking that this is so. This is a *reliabilist* approach to the epistemology of instruments, and it can be applied to the domain of testimony equally easily. In the same way that an instrument can put an observer in a position to know something by producing reliable deliverances, a speaker can put a listener in a position to know something by producing reliable testimony.[12]

Not everyone believes that instruments and testimony are similar sources of knowledge in this way, though. According to some, testimony can put a listener in a position to know what the speaker says in a way that instruments cannot. The reason is that a knowledgeable speaker is able not only to allow the listener *to know what she knows* but also to allow the listener *to acquire her knowledge*. Instruments, in virtue of not knowing things in the way that speakers do, cannot do this. This is what is meant by knowledge transmission.

What does the transmission of knowledge involve? John Greco (2016) helpfully distinguishes two answers. According to one, the transmission of knowledge involves nothing more than a listener coming to know that φ by believing the testimony (that φ) of a speaker who knows that φ. As Greco points out, any theory that allows that testimony can put a listener in a position to know what a speaker says endorses knowledge transmission in this sense (Greco 2016, p. 481). We might call this the *weak* sense of transmission.

Greco also identifies a stronger notion of transmission. There are those who maintain that 'there is a special kind of knowledge transmission that occurs in at least some testimonial exchanges, and that it cannot be understood in terms of these familiar epistemic categories' (Greco 2016, p. 482). Now, Greco is correct that there are more substantive notions of transmission available than the weak sense outlined above, though a still more fine-grained taxonomy of transmission theorists is in order.

In addition to cases in which a speaker's testimony can put a listener in a position to know what she knows, it is plausible that there are also cases in which a listener coming to know depends on the speaker knowing. If I tell you that Marie Curie was born in 1867 and you reason that not easily would I say this unless I knew it, your knowledge depends on me knowing what I say. If I do not know it, then your belief is based on a falsehood that, intuitively, prevents you from knowing.[13] One might conceive of transmission in terms of a listener's knowledge depending on the speaker knowing what she says. We might call this the moderate sense of transmission.[14]

There is, however, a stronger sense of knowledge transmission. Elucidating it requires bringing into view an idea of epistemic grounds. For the purpose of this discussion, epistemic grounds can be understood as that which puts someone in a position to know. Intuitively, if you encounter a production of Shakespeare's *Othello* taking place in the park and I do not, then you are in a position to know that such a production is taking place and I am not. The reason is that encountering it provides you with something that I do not have – epistemic grounds.[15]

The disagreement between the internalist and reliabilist approaches to testimony outlined above can be thought of as a disagreement over the epistemic grounds that underpin knowledge from testimony. The internalist approach maintains that a listener is in a position to know what a speaker says because of the reasons that she is aware of. The reliabilist approach maintains that a listener is in a position to know what a speaker says because of the reliability of the speaker's testimony. This amounts to a disagreement over epistemic grounds.

This is not to say that all subjects who have epistemic grounds for what they believe thereby have knowledge. The subjects in the plenitudinous array of Gettier cases fail to know what they believe. In the case where the subject believes that either Jones owns a Ford or Brown is in Barcelona, the subject fails to know because her reasons that she is aware of are not good enough, or the process by which she forms her belief lacks the relevant property, or she is unable to use the relevant fact as a reason, or her mental state is non-factive. Something similar is true of the subject who sees a barn in a field full of facsimiles, or the subject who sees the stopped clock, or the subject who sees a sheep-shaped object that she takes to be a sheep.

Whichever way the relevant point is spelled out, the problem is a short-coming of their epistemic grounds. Accounting for what that shortcoming amounts to might be difficult, impossible or entirely wrongheaded. The point is that some deficiency prevents them from knowing, and this is a deficiency concerning their epistemic grounds. With this in mind, we can turn to consider knowledge transmission in its strongest sense.

The strong sense of knowledge transmission is grounded in a more fundamental notion – the transmission of epistemic grounds. What does this involve? Tyler Burge (1993, 1997, 2013) provides an influential answer.[16] Burge's account of transmission is buried in a complex distinction between justifications and entitlements.[17] For the purpose of this discussion, we can bypass these complexities and get straight to the core of the issue.

In a situation where a speaker tells a listener that ϕ, there are two sets of epistemic grounds for ϕ. There are the speaker's epistemic grounds for ϕ, and there are the listener's epistemic grounds for ϕ. Of course, either or both sets may be empty. But Burge's idea is that, when the speaker tells the listener that ϕ, the speaker's epistemic grounds for ϕ are added to the listener's prior epistemic grounds for ϕ. The listener thus acquires the speaker's epistemic grounds. In a case where this brings the listener to know that ϕ, the listener's knowledge that ϕ is grounded not only in her previous epistemic grounds for ϕ, but also in the speaker's epistemic grounds for ϕ.

To take an example, suppose I tell you that the LA Rams lost 44–6 to the Arizona Cardinals. You may already be aware that the Rams have a number of injuries and the Cardinals do not. You thus have some epistemic grounds for believing what I say. There are also my epistemic grounds for believing what I say, such as my having been at the game and seen it. The idea is that, when I tell you that the Rams lost 44–6 to the Cardinals, my epistemic grounds are made available to you. If you come to know by taking me at my word, your knowledge can be underpinned by my epistemic grounds.

Of course, exactly what this amounts to might depend on how we think about epistemic grounds, and that, in turn, might depend on how we think about knowledge. The central idea, though, should be clear enough. Burge's account of the transmission of epistemic grounds is, I believe, largely correct. There are, however, two further refinements that are important. Instead of thinking of the transmission of epistemic grounds simply in terms of the listener acquiring the speaker's epistemic grounds for what she says, I propose the following account:

(TG) The transmission of epistemic grounds is a matter of a subject's epistemic grounds for ϕ becoming the listener's epistemic grounds for ϕ, in virtue of the fact that they are the subject's epistemic grounds for ϕ.[18]

Two points are immediately important about **(TG)**. First, it refers to a speaker's epistemic grounds becoming a listener's epistemic grounds *in virtue of* the fact that they are the speaker's epistemic grounds. Second, it does not refer to the speaker telling the listener that ϕ, or asserting that ϕ, or even saying that ϕ. These two points seem trivial, but they are important to understanding what the transmission of epistemic grounds involves.

Suppose I see a sign saying that the Queen's Lane Coffee House will be closing at 3pm today. I therefore have some epistemic grounds for thinking that the Queen's Lane Coffee House will be closing at 3pm today. Suppose that you later see the same sign. We might think that the epistemology of signs is such that, on the assumption that you and I have no additional information relevant to the closing time of the Queen's Lane Coffee House, you and I have the same epistemic grounds for thinking that the Queen's Lane Coffee House will close today at 3pm.

In this situation, my epistemic grounds for thinking that the Queen's Lane Coffee House will be closing at 3pm today become your grounds for thinking this. However, this is intuitively not a case of the transmission of epistemic grounds. The reason for this is that the fact that these epistemic grounds are my epistemic grounds has nothing to do with the fact that they become your epistemic grounds. As you saw the sign independently, it is not true that you would not have had these epistemic grounds had I not had them, nor the case that you have them because I have them. Whilst my epistemic grounds become your epistemic grounds, it is not the case that this happens in virtue of them being my epistemic grounds.

This is why **(TG)** appeals to the speaker's epistemic grounds becoming the listener's epistemic grounds in virtue of the fact that they are the speaker's epistemic grounds. The idea of the transmission of epistemic grounds is supposed to capture something much more particular than what goes on in the case where you and I see the same sign. The point about there being no reference to the speaker saying anything is also important. Throughout this discussion, I shall focus primarily on cases in which epistemic grounds are transmitted through a speaker's testimony, but this is not strictly necessary for the transmission of epistemic grounds.

Sanford Goldberg (2010) has argued – to my mind convincingly – that silence can be a source of knowledge. The idea is that someone might come to know that ϕ on the grounds that, if ϕ was not true, then a would-be speaker would have said something. For example, suppose that you and I are in DC trying to get to the Woodrow Wilson Memorial and I express my belief that we should take the road to the left by saying this aloud. If you say nothing, then this, in the right circumstances, might allow me to know that I am right.

What, then, grounds knowledge that is acquired in this way? The obvious answers correspond to the answers to the question of what grounds knowledge acquired by believing testimony. Knowledge acquired through silence might be grounded in my reasons for thinking that, if we should not take the road to the left, then you would have said something, or your reliable tendency to intervene, or your epistemic grounds for what I say becoming my epistemic grounds.

Goldberg's discussion convinces me that silence can be a source of knowledge in the same way that testimony can. Since I think that testimony can transmit epistemic grounds, I also think that silence can transmit epistemic grounds. Thus, whilst I shall focus on the transmission of epistemic grounds through testimony, I intend everything that I say about a speaker's testimony that ϕ to be applicable *mutatis mutandis* to a speaker's silence with respect to ϕ.

Transmission theorists are given to thinking about the acquisition of epistemic grounds through transmission as something similar to the acquisition of other goods. Thinking about the acquisition of someone's collection of ancient Roman coins helps elucidate this point. If I have a collection of 71 ancient Roman coins, then you can acquire at most 71 ancient Roman coins from me. More generally, you cannot acquire more ancient Roman coins from me than I have. A corollary is that, if I have *no* ancient Roman coins, then you cannot acquire any from me.

An interesting question concerns whether or not a listener could acquire *part* of someone's epistemic grounds for what she says through transmission. If I have 71 ancient Roman coins, then it is possible for me to give you some of them, thus resulting in you acquiring, say, 67 ancient Roman coins from me. Is something similar true of transmission? I believe that it is not, as we shall see in §2.3.

The fact that you can only acquire up to 71 Roman coins *from me* is also important. This does *not*, however, entail that you cannot come to have more than 71 coins yourself, by acquiring mine. You might have already had some of your own, which are supplemented by the ones that you acquire from me, or you might simultaneously acquire some from elsewhere, giving you more than 71 as a result. The fact that I have 71 ancient Roman coins thus does not entail that you cannot come to have more than 71 by acquiring mine. Nor does it entail that your acquisition of my coins is not part of the explanation of how you came to have the number you do. It *does*, however, entail that you coming to have more than 71 coins by acquiring mine must involve you also acquiring some from another source.

Using the account of the transmission of epistemic grounds given in **(TG)**, we can develop an account of the strong sense of knowledge transmission, which is the sense that will be the primary subject of the discussion:

(TK) The transmission of knowledge that φ involves the listener coming to know that φ in virtue of the transmission of epistemic grounds from a subject who knows that φ.

This account of knowledge transmission is built on the above account of the transmission of epistemic grounds. The account of the transmission of epistemic grounds is therefore fundamental in two ways. First, it is fundamental *conceptually*, in that the transmission of epistemic grounds is not defined in terms of the transmission of knowledge, but the transmission of knowledge is defined in terms of the transmission of epistemic grounds. It is also fundamental *epistemically*, in that the transmission of epistemic grounds is a necessary condition of the transmission of knowledge, but the transmission of knowledge is not a necessary condition of the transmission of epistemic grounds.

At first sight, this might appear strange. The logic of knowledge and epistemic grounds might seem to impugn the claim that epistemic grounds can be transmitted without knowledge being transmitted but not vice versa.[19] The fact that a listener knows that a speaker knows something entails that the listener is in a position to know it. Yet the fact that a listener knows that a speaker has epistemic grounds for something does not entail that the listener has epistemic grounds for it. This would seem to indicate that knowledge is somehow *more* commonable than epistemic grounds, but the relationship between them given here maintains that the reverse is true.

Here is an example that illustrates the idea that knowledge is more commonable than epistemic grounds: Suppose that a speaker tells a listener that there are no fake barns in the vicinity. The listener knows that the speaker has seen a sign saying that all the nearby fake barns have been removed and thus has epistemic grounds for what she says. The listener also knows, however, that there are various misleading signs in the vicinity and that the speaker is unable to distinguish between the accurate ones and the misleading ones.

In this situation, the listener might know that the speaker has epistemic grounds for thinking that there are no fake barns in the vicinity, but nonetheless she does not have epistemic grounds for this herself. The fact that the listener is aware that the speaker has seen a sign means that she knows that the speaker has epistemic grounds for what she says. However, the fact that the listener knows that there are misleading signs nearby and that the speaker cannot distinguish accurate signs from misleading signs means that the listener herself does not have epistemic grounds for thinking that there are no fake barns in the vicinity. Her knowledge that there are some misleading signs and that the speaker is unable to distinguish between accurate ones and misleading ones defeats any epistemic grounds that she might have.[20]

The logic of knowledge and epistemic grounds might thus make the claim that epistemic grounds can be transmitted without knowledge being transmitted, but not the reverse, surprising. In this case, however, focusing on the logic of knowledge and epistemic grounds is apt to mislead us. What matters is that having epistemic grounds for ϕ does not entail knowing that ϕ, or being in a position to know that ϕ. By contrast, knowing that ϕ does entail having epistemic grounds for ϕ. As we shall see, this is important to understanding what kinds of considerations count against transmission theories.

We now have an initial account of the transmission of epistemic grounds in view, which in turn gives rise to an initial account of the transmission of knowledge, in the strong sense. These two accounts, along with observations about the relationship between them, will provide the foundations for the following discussion.

Notes

1 See John McDowell (1982, 1995, 2002).
2 See Laurence BonJour (1985), Keith Lehrer (2000) and Richard Fumerton (1995).
3 Compare Stewart Cohen (1998) and Keith DeRose (2009) with John Hawthorne (2004) and Jason Stanley (2005).
4 See Alvin Goldman (1967). Cf. Goldman (1976).
5 See William Alston (1996), Alvin Goldman (2012) and David Papineau (1992).
6 See Sosa (2007, 2009). Duncan Pritchard (2012) suggests this but also states that it must be one that manifests the subject's abilities.
7 See Kelly Becker (2007), Fred Dretske (1970) and Robert Nozick (1981).
8 The most prominent defender of this view is Tim Williamson (2000).
9 See John Hyman (2015). Cf. Kenny (1989), Ryle (1949) and White (1982).
10 A lot of things, anyway. Some things, like moral or aesthetic matters, might not be knowable on the basis of testimony. See Roger Crisp (2014), Alison Hills (2009), Rob Hopkins (2007, 2011), Robert J. Howell (2014) and Sarah McGrath (2009).

11 Joseph Shieber (2015) has an excellent discussion of Locke's views on testimony.

12 Ernest Sosa (2010) provides the most explicit endorsement of this type of approach.

13 This thought is manifested in Elizabeth Fricker's (2006) discussion.

14 Fricker's (2015) theory is a transmission theory in the moderate sense.

15 Some philosophers think of epistemic grounds in terms of *justification*. The trouble is, however, that not everyone agrees. Internalists do, but reliabilists are less clear. Robert Audi (2006) and Hilary Kornblith (2008), for example, do not. Alvin Goldman vacillates between the two – compare Goldman (1967) and (1976) with Goldman (1979). For the sake of clarity, then, I shall eschew talk of justification in favour of talk of epistemic grounds.

16 The core idea behind Burge's account has been developed up by Edward Hinchman (2005) and Paul Faulkner (2011) amongst others.

17 On Burge's distinction between justifications and entitlements, see Peter Graham (2010), Anna-Sara Malmgren (2006) and Ram Neta (2010). For contrasting accounts of entitlements, see Fred Dretske (2000) and Crispin Wright (2004).

18 This is a refinement of the account of the transmission of epistemic grounds I have given in Stephen Wright (2015, 2016a, 2016b).

19 In this spirit, see Jaakko Hintikka's (2005) discussion of the logic of knowledge and belief and Michael Welbourne's (1986) discussion of the commonability of knowledge.

20 On the subject of defeaters, see Pollock (1974).

Bibliography

Alston, W. (1996). *The Reliability of Sense Perception*. Ithaca, NY: Cornell University Press.

Audi, R. (2006). Testimony, credulity, and veracity. In J. Lackey and E. Sosa (Eds.), *The Epistemology of Testimony*, pp. 25–49. Oxford: Oxford University Press.

Becker, K. (2007). *Epistemology Modalized*. London: Routledge.

BonJour, L. (1985). *The Structure of Empirical Knowledge*. Cambridge, MA: Harvard University Press.

Burge, T. (1993). Content preservation. *Philosophical Review* 102(4), 457–488.

Burge, T. (1997). Interlocution, perception, and memory. *Philosophical Studies* 86(1), 21–47.

Burge, T. (2013). Postscript: Content preservation. In T. Burge (Ed.), *Cognition Through Understanding: Self-Knowledge, Interlocution, Reasoning, Reflection: Philosophical Essays Volume 3*. Oxford: Oxford University Press.

Cohen, S. (1998). Contextualist solutions to epistemological problems: Scepticism, Gettier and the lottery. *Australasian Journal of Philosophy* 76(2), 289–306.

Crisp, R. (2014). Moral testimony pessimism: A defence. *Proceedings of the Aristotelian Society Supplementary Volume* 88(1), 129–143.

DeRose, K. (2009). *The Case for Contextualism*. Oxford: Oxford University Press.

Dretske, F. (1970). Epistemic operators. *Journal of Philosophy* 67(24), 1007–1023.

Dretske, F. (2000). Entitlement: Epistemic rights without epistemic duties? *Philosophy and Phenomenological Research* 60(3), 591–606.

Faulkner, P. (2011). *Knowledge on Trust*. Oxford: Oxford University Press.

Fricker, E. (2006). Second-hand knowledge. *Philosophy and Phenomenological Research* 73(3), 592–618.

Fricker, E. (2015). How to make invidious distinctions amongst reliable testifiers. *Episteme* 12(2), 173–202.

Fumerton, R. (1995). *Metaepistemology and Scepticism*. London: Rowman & Littlefield.

Goldberg, S. (2010). *Relying on Others*. Oxford: Oxford University Press.

Goldman, A. (1967). A causal theory of knowing. *Journal of Philosophy* 64(12), 357–372.

Goldman, A. (1976). Discrimination and perceptual knowledge. *Journal of Philosophy* 73(11), 771–791.

Goldman, A. (1979). What is justified belief? In G. Pappas (Ed.), *Knowledge and Justification*, pp. 1–23. Dordrecht: D. Reidel Publishing Company.

Goldman, A. (2012). *Reliabilism and Contemporary Epistemology*. Oxford: Oxford University Press.

Graham, P. (2010). Testimonial entitlement and the function of comprehension. In A. Haddock, A. Millar and D. Pritchard (Eds.), *Social Epistemology*, pp. 148–174. Oxford: Oxford University Press.

Greco, J. (2016). What is transmission*? *Episteme* 13(4), 481–498.

Hills, A. (2009). Moral testimony and moral epistemology. *Ethics* 120(1), 94–127.

Hinchman, E. (2005). Telling as inviting to trust. *Philosophy and Phenomenological Research* 70(3), 562–587.

Hintikka, J. (2005). *Knowledge and Belief: An Introduction to the Logic of the Two Notions*. London: King's College Publications.

Hopkins, R. (2007). What is wrong with moral testimony. *Philosophy and Phenomenological Research* 74(3), 611–634.

Hopkins, R. (2011). How to be a pessimist about aesthetic testimony. *Journal of Philosophy* 108(3), 138–157.

Howell, R. J. (2014). Google morals, virtue, and the asymmetry of deference. *Noûs* 48(3), 389–415.

Hyman, J. (2015). *Action, Knowledge, and Will*. Oxford: Oxford University Press.

Kenny, A. (1989). *The Metaphysics of Mind*. Oxford: Oxford University Press.

Kornblith, H. (2008). Knowledge needs no justification. In Q. Smith (Ed.), *Epistemology: New Essays*, pp. 5–23. Oxford: Oxford University Press.

Lehrer, K. (2000). *Theory of Knowledge*, second edition. Boulder: Westview Press.

Locke, J. (1689). *An Essay Concerning Human Understanding*. London: Rivington.

Malmgren, A. S. (2006). Is there a priori knowledge by testimony? *Philosophical Review* 115(2), 199–241.

McDowell, J. (1982). Criteria, defeasibility, and knowledge. *Proceedings of the British Academy* 68, 435–479.

McDowell, J. (1995). Knowledge and the internal. *Philosophy and Phenomenological Research* 55(4), 877–893.

McDowell, J. (2002). Knowledge and the internal revisited. *Philosophy and Phenomenological Research* 64(1), 97–105.

McGrath, S. (2009). The puzzle of pure moral deference. *Philosophical Perspectives* 23(1), 321–344.

Neta, R. (2010). Can a priori entitlement be preserved by testimony. In A. Haddock, A. Millar and D. Pritchard (Eds.), *Social Epistemology*. Oxford: Oxford University Press.

Nozick, R. (1981). *Philosophical Explanations*. Oxford: Oxford University Press.

Papineau, D. (1992). Reliabilism, induction and scepticism. *Philosophical Quarterly* 42(1), 1–20.

Pollock, J. (1974). *Knowledge and Justification*. Princeton, NJ: Princeton University Press.

Pritchard, D. (2012). Anti-luck virtue epistemology. *Journal of Philosophy* 109(3), 247–279.

Ryle, G. (1949). *The Concept of Mind*. Chicago: University of Chicago Press.

Shieber, J. (2015). *Testimony: A Philosophical Introduction*. London: Routledge.

Sosa, E. (2007). *A Virtue Epistemology: Apt Belief and Reflective Knowledge, Volume 1*. Oxford: Oxford University Press.

Sosa, E. (2009). *A Virtue Epistemology: Apt Belief and Reflective Knowledge, Volume 2*. Oxford: Oxford University Press.

Sosa, E. (2010). *Knowing Full Well*. Princeton, NJ: Princeton University Press.

Stanley, J. (2005). *Knowledge and Practical Interests*. Oxford: Oxford University Press.

Welbourne, M. (1986). *Community of Knowledge*. Aberdeen: Aberdeen University Press.

White, A. R. (1982). *The Nature of Knowledge*. Totowa: Rowman & Littlefield.

Williamson, T. (2000). *Knowledge and its Limits*. Oxford: Oxford University Press.

Wright, C. (2004). Warrant for nothing (and foundations for free)? *Aristotelian Society Supplementary Volume* 78(1), 167–212.

Wright, S. (2015). In defence of transmission. *Episteme* 12(1), 13–28.

Wright, S. (2016a). Sincerity and transmission. *Ratio* 29(1), 42–56.

Wright, S. (2016b). The transmission of knowledge and justification. *Synthese* 193(1), 293–311.

2 Availability

2.1 Introduction

We have seen that knowing that ϕ is a matter of standing in a certain relationship to the fact that ϕ. The question is how a speaker's testimony can put a listener in a position to know that ϕ. One way is through the transmission of epistemic grounds, as described in the previous chapter. The transmission of epistemic grounds involves two things. First, it involves the speaker making her epistemic grounds available to a listener. Second, it involves the listener successfully acquiring those epistemic grounds.[1] In this chapter, we shall focus on the first issue. Since we have already seen that the transmission of epistemic grounds is the more fundamental notion, we shall begin with the transmission of epistemic grounds.

Existing transmission theories endorse one of the following two principles concerning the availability of epistemic grounds:

(TG-N₁) A speaker's testimony that ϕ can make epistemic grounds for ϕ available to transmit to a listener only if the speaker has epistemic grounds for ϕ.[2]

(TG-N₂) A speaker's testimony that ϕ can make epistemic grounds for ϕ available to transmit to a listener only if some speaker in the testimonial chain has epistemic grounds for ϕ.[3]

Both **(TG-N₁)** and **(TG-N₂)** maintain that someone in the testimonial chain having epistemic grounds for ϕ is a necessary condition of a speaker's testimony that ϕ making epistemic grounds for ϕ available to transmit. This, I shall argue, is incorrect. As a result, instead of **(TG-N₁)** or **(TG-N₂)**, I endorse the following claim:

(TG-N₃) A speaker's testimony that ϕ can make epistemic grounds for ϕ available to transmit to a listener only if someone has epistemic grounds for ϕ.

Unlike (**TG-N₁**) and (**TG-N₂**), (**TG-N₃**) does not maintain that someone in the testimonial chain having epistemic grounds for φ is a necessary condition of a speaker's testimony that φ making epistemic grounds for φ available to transmit. Rather, (**TG-N₃**) maintains only that someone – who may or may not be in the testimonial chain – having epistemic grounds for φ is a necessary condition of a speaker's testimony that φ making epistemic grounds for φ available to transmit.

In an important sense, the dispute over the above principles is a secondary one. The primary issue concerns what a speaker has to do in order to make epistemic grounds available to transmit to a listener. In this chapter, I shall argue that the speaker's testimony making epistemic grounds available to transmit to a listener is a matter of the speaker's testimony being sincere in a particular sense.

2.2 Sincerity

Suppose a speaker tells a listener that the Battle of Leuctra took place in the year 371 BC because she realises that this is what the evidence best supports. The speaker herself, however, does not believe this because she has been trying to convince herself that the Battle of Leuctra really took place in the year 371 AD, as a result of having just written it in an examination. Nonetheless, she tells the listener that the Battle of Leuctra took place in the year 371 BC because she realises that this is what the evidence best supports.[4]

Is the speaker's testimony in this case sincere? In one sense, the answer is clearly no. The speaker does not believe what she says, and this clearly rules it out from being sincere.[5] In another sense, however, the speaker's testimony is sincere. Compare this speaker with one who tells the listener that the Battle of Leuctra took place in the year 371 BC not because of any epistemic considerations, but because she believes that the listener is uninterested in battles that took place before the year 1 AD, and so by saying it took place in 371 BC she is hoping that the listener will go away. Whilst neither speaker's testimony is sincere in one sense of the term, there is a sense in which the former speaker's testimony is sincere where the latter speaker's testimony is not.

Since neither speaker believes what she says, we might say that neither speaker's testimony is *doxastically sincere*. However, the former speaker's testimony is connected to her epistemic grounds in a particular way, where the latter speaker's testimony is not. We might say, then, that the former speaker's testimony is *epistemically sincere*, whereas the latter speaker's testimony is not. Epistemic sincerity might be characterised in the following way:

(**ES**) A speaker's testimony that φ is epistemically sincere if and only if, for someone's epistemic grounds, the fact that they are epistemic grounds for φ is the reason why the speaker said that φ.[6]

What is meant by the fact that some epistemic grounds are epistemic grounds for φ being the reason why a speaker said that φ? More generally, what is meant by anything being the reason why anything else? John Hyman's (2015) discussion of knowledge that φ as the ability to be guided by the fact that φ is instructive here.[7]

To say that a set of epistemic grounds is epistemic grounds for φ is the reason why the speaker said that φ is to say that the fact that a set of epistemic grounds is epistemic grounds for φ *explains why* the speaker said that φ. There are two important parts to this. First, it must be that the speaker knows that the epistemic grounds are epistemic grounds for φ. Second, it must be that the fact that the epistemic grounds are epistemic grounds for φ that guides the speaker in saying that φ.

Given the differences between the ordinary notion of sincerity – that of doxastic sincerity – and the notion of epistemic sincerity given in (**ES**), one might wonder why we should think of epistemic sincerity as a species of sincerity at all. In one sense, whether we regard epistemic sincerity as being of the same genus as doxastic sincerity is unimportant – what matters is what epistemic sincerity amounts to. But there is an important sense in which they are similar.

Both doxastic sincerity and epistemic sincerity involve being in a position to vouch for what one says. In the case of doxastic sincerity, a speaker vouches for what she says by reference to the fact that she believes what she says. In the case of epistemic sincerity, a speaker vouches for what she says by reference to the epistemic grounds that support what she says. And in the same way that the mere fact that one believes what one says does not make one's statement doxastically sincere – the fact that one believes it must be the reason why one says it – the mere fact that there are epistemic grounds for what one says does not make one's statement epistemically sincere – the epistemic grounds must be the reason why one says it.

These two points can be illustrated using the example of a speaker telling a listener about the Battle of Leuctra. Consider the speaker whose testimony is epistemically sincere. The idea is that the fact her evidence constitutes epistemic grounds for φ is the reason why she says that φ. This entails that she knows that φ. Why? Suppose it was not the case that she knew this, either because it was not true or because her belief in it failed to amount to knowledge. In either case, it would seem intuitive that the reason why she said that φ was because she *believed* that the epistemic grounds were epistemic grounds for φ, rather than the *fact* that the epistemic grounds were epistemic grounds for φ.[8]

Now, this is not to say that, in such a case, the fact that the epistemic grounds were epistemic grounds for φ could not be the speaker's motivation for saying that φ.[9] She might have intended to use the fact that the epistemic grounds are epistemic grounds for φ as the reason why she said that φ, but she is unable to. In the case where the epistemic grounds are not epistemic grounds for φ, her saying that φ cannot be explained in terms of the epistemic grounds being epistemic grounds for φ, because this is false and falsehoods do not explain. In the case where her belief fails to amount to knowledge, she does not have the right kind of access to the fact for it to explain her speech act.[10]

The fact that the speaker knows that the epistemic grounds are epistemic grounds for φ, however, does not by itself entail that this fact is the reason why the speaker says that φ. Rather, the fact must guide the speaker's act of saying that φ in the right way. Hyman's way of expressing this idea is in terms of the fact being a fact in the light of which the agent did the act being explained, a fact that guided her when she did it (Hyman 2015, p. 137). Reducing this notion is difficult, but Hyman gives a couple of examples of what it is to be guided by something. The example of a cat modifying its behaviour when stalking a bird is one. The cat responds to the bird's movements and so is being guided by the bird. An alternative example involves a traveller following a guide – as the guide takes the road to the left, the traveller follows (Hyman 2015, p. 169).[11]

The unifying idea is that being guided by something involves being responsive to it. Whilst giving a reductive analysis is difficult, it is important to distinguish the notion of being responsive to a fact from notions of *safety* and *sensitivity* as they appear in the philosophical literature. As a property of beliefs, safety is understood as a matter of how easily the processes involved in the production of the belief might have yielded a false belief. In terms of possible worlds, safety is a matter of how far away the nearest possible world is in which the processes return a false belief. A belief being sensitive involves the belief being such that, if its content were not true, then the subject would not believe it, whereas if its content were true, then the subject would believe it. Again, in terms of possible worlds, it is a matter of the subject not believing what she does in the nearest possible world in which the content of her belief is false and still believing it in the nearest possible world in which it is true.

It might be natural to think that the idea of being responsive to a fact, or being guided by a fact, can be reduced into one of these two notions. Someone's action being guided by the fact that φ might involve there being no close possible world in which she acts, but φ is not the case. Alternatively, it might involve being such that in the closest possible world where she acts, φ is the case, and in the closest possible world in which she does not, φ is not the case. However, there is more to being responsive to something, or to being guided by something, than safety and sensitivity.

In order to see this, consider a case in which both you and I are being guided by the same guide. As the guide takes the road to the left, so do we. As the guide continues on ahead, we follow. We are both responsive to the guide's movements, but neither of us is responding to the other. This, however, is at odds with thinking of being guided by something in terms of being sensitive to it. In the nearest possible world in which you turn to the right, I turn to the right, and in the nearest possible world in which you do not, neither do I. In both cases, this is because we are being guided by the guide and this is the direction that the guide takes us in; it is not because we are being guided by each other.

Something similar is true of safety. It might well be the case that the closest possible world in which you go one way, but I go another, is far off. Yet this does not mean that either of us is being guided by, or is responding to, the other. Rather, we are both being guided by the same guide. We should therefore refrain from reducing the idea of being guided to either safety or sensitivity.

Even in its unreduced state, the idea of something being the reason why a speaker said that ϕ can still be informative. We have seen that epistemic sincerity requires, at a minimum, the speaker knowing that a set of epistemic grounds is epistemic grounds for what she says and being responsive to this fact in deciding to say what she does. In the case where the speaker's testimony about the Battle of Leuctra is epistemically sincere, we can see why this is the case. We can see that the speaker recognises that the evidence best supports the proposition that the Battle of Leuctra took place in the year 371 BC and tells the listener this because she recognises this.

From the conception of epistemic sincerity, the conditions under which a speaker's testimony makes epistemic grounds for what she says available to transmit are straightforward:

(TG-N)   A speaker's testimony that ϕ can make epistemic grounds for ϕ available to transmit to a listener if and only if the speaker's testimony that ϕ is epistemically sincere.[12]

Why should we accept **(TG-N)** as an account of the conditions under which a speaker's testimony makes epistemic grounds available to transmit? The answer comes in two parts. The first purports to establish the necessity of epistemic sincerity; the second purports to establish the sufficiency of epistemic sincerity. This will be the subject of §2.3. For the time being, let us conclude the overview of **(TG-N)** by examining its relationship to the principles **(TG-N$_1$)**, **(TG-N$_2$)** and **(TG-N$_3$)** respectively.

(TG-N) is incompatible with both **(TG-N$_1$)** and **(TG-N$_2$)**. To see this, consider a case in which a speaker tells a listener that Handel wrote 29 oratorios because she knows that a third party has epistemic grounds for believing this. The speaker herself has grounds to doubt the reliability of the third party's sources, but she tells the listener that Handel wrote 29 oratorios because she believes that she ought to tell the listener whatever the third party's epistemic grounds best support – for example, because she knows that the listener always believes the third party's evidence to be unimpeachable.

The speaker's testimony is epistemically sincere. She says that Handel wrote 29 oratorios because this is what the third party's epistemic grounds indicate. The speaker recognises that the third party's epistemic grounds are epistemic grounds for thinking that Handel wrote 29 oratorios and so she says that Handel wrote 29 oratorios. However, neither the speaker nor anyone else in the testimonial chain has epistemic grounds for what the speaker says. The speaker's grounds for doubting the reliability of the third party's sources defeat her epistemic grounds, and there is nobody else in the testimonial chain.

This is why **(TG-N)** is incompatible with both **(TG-N₁)** and **(TG-N₂)**. By contrast, **(TG-N)** is not only compatible with **(TG-N₃)** but *entails* **(TG-N₃)**. If nobody has epistemic grounds for what the speaker says, then the speaker's testimony cannot make epistemic grounds available to transmit. The statement of epistemic sincerity in **(ES)** requires that the speaker says what she does because someone's epistemic grounds support what she says. This, however, depends on someone's epistemic grounds being epistemic grounds for what the speaker says. If nobody has epistemic grounds for what the speaker says, the speaker's testimony cannot be epistemically sincere.

Furthermore, as we saw in Chapter 1, the basic idea behind the transmission of epistemic grounds involves a subject's epistemic grounds becoming a listener's epistemic grounds. A necessary condition of this is that some subject has epistemic grounds that can be transmitted, as **(TG-N₃)** states. Hence, the basic idea behind the transmission of epistemic grounds set out in **(TG)** is also a logical consequence of **(TG-N₃)**.

2.3   The availability of epistemic grounds

The claim in **(TG-N)** is therefore important. With this in mind, let us turn to the question of why anyone should think that **(TG-N)** is true. According to **(TG-N)**, a speaker's testimony being epistemically sincere is both necessary and sufficient for her testimony making epistemic grounds available to transmit. As noted in §2.2, the argument for this comes in two stages. The first establishes the necessity of epistemic sincerity; the second establishes its sufficiency.

In support of the idea that epistemic sincerity is necessary for a speaker's testimony making epistemic grounds available to transmit, consider a case in which a speaker's testimony is not epistemically sincere. Suppose that Alice tells Ellen that the bank closes at 4pm today because she knows this and wants to inform her. Ellen does not believe Alice, but when she subsequently sees Sarah, she tells her that the bank closes at 4pm because she believes that it will upset her.

Does Ellen's testimony make epistemic grounds available to Sarah? According to the view given in **(TG-N)**, it does not. But other transmission theorists maintain that it does, specifically Burge (1993) and Faulkner (2011). According to Faulkner, the fact that Alice knows what she says and intends to inform Ellen means that Ellen's subsequent testimony makes epistemic grounds available to transmit to Sarah. Specifically, the epistemic grounds that it makes available to transmit are Alice's epistemic grounds for what she says (Faulkner 2011, p. 61). Thinking about the case in this way motivates **(TG-N$_2$)** and, in doing so, provides a reason for rejecting **(TG-N)**.

This case, however, falls short of undermining **(TG-N)**. The main reason is that it is unclear why we should think that Ellen's testimony makes epistemic grounds available to transmit to Sarah. The case against **(TG-N)** depends on this claim, but there are reasons for doubting it. The idea behind the reasons for doubting that Ellen's testimony makes Alice's epistemic grounds available to Sarah is that, regardless of how strong Alice's epistemic grounds are, Ellen's testimony intuitively does not put Sarah in a position to know that the bank closes at 4pm. That is to say that Sarah cannot, by believing Ellen's testimony, come to know the truth of what she says. As we saw in Chapter 1, knowing that ϕ is a matter of having the right kind of access to ϕ, and Ellen's testimony cannot provide Sarah with that kind of access to the fact that ϕ.

For Ellen's testimony to provide Sarah with the kind of access to the fact that the bank closes at 4pm required for her to be in a position to know this, it needs to be the case that Ellen's testimony is somehow connected to the fact that the bank closes at 4pm. In a case where a speaker's testimony that ϕ is epistemically sincere, the fact that someone's epistemic grounds are epistemic grounds for ϕ is the reason why she says that ϕ. What is more, the fact that someone's epistemic grounds are epistemic grounds for ϕ, combined with the fact that this is the reason why the speaker says that ϕ, establishes a connection between the fact that ϕ and the speaker's testimony that ϕ.[13]

Knowledge that ϕ, as we saw in Chapter 1, is a matter of being related to the fact that ϕ in the right way. Whatever that way amounts to, Sarah cannot come to be related to the fact that the bank closes at 4pm by believing Ellen's testimony, as Ellen's testimony has nothing to do with the fact that the bank closes at 4pm. This is because the reason why she says it is not the fact that the bank closes at 4pm, nor is it the fact that this is what her epistemic grounds best support. Rather, the reason why she says it is that she believes that it will upset Sarah. Insofar as she knows that this is the case, the reason why she says it might be the fact that it will upset Sarah. But, it has nothing to do with the fact that she reports, or any epistemic grounds for it.

Whilst it might be true that the fact that the bank closes at 4pm is the reason why Alice says this, it cannot be the reason why Ellen says this. Whilst it is true that Ellen repeats to Sarah a claim that Alice made because the bank closes at 4pm, Ellen's decision to tell Sarah this is indifferent to the truth of whether or not the bank actually closes at 4pm. Rather, it is made because of how believing that the bank closes at 4pm will affect Sarah. Hence, the fact that the bank closes at 4pm is not the reason why Ellen says that the bank closes at 4pm.

Ellen's testimony cannot therefore bring about the kind of relationship between Sarah and the fact that the bank closes at 4pm that is required for Sarah to be in a position to know this. Another way of putting this is in terms of the epistemic basing relation. The idea behind the epistemic basing relation is straightforward enough. It is the relationship that holds between a belief and a set of epistemic grounds where the belief is supported by – or based on – the epistemic grounds. Exactly what this amounts to, though, is very hard to spell out.[14] According to some, it amounts to a causal relation.[15] Another approach takes it to be a counterfactual relation.[16] A different approach takes it to be a matter of the subject having certain dispositions.[17]

Whilst the details of the epistemic basing relation are unclear, it might nonetheless help us to elucidate the idea that Ellen's testimony does not make Alice's epistemic grounds available to Sarah. Sarah's belief being based on Alice's epistemic grounds depends on Sarah's belief being connected to Alice's epistemic grounds in a particular way. For Ellen's testimony to make Alice's epistemic grounds available to Sarah in this way, her testimony needs to make it the case that Sarah, in believing her testimony, can form a belief that is connected to Alice's epistemic grounds in the relevant way. In the case in question, this is not plausibly so. Alice's epistemic grounds have nothing to do with Ellen's testimony, since both the reason why she tells Sarah that the bank closes at 4pm and her motivation for doing so are either her belief that it will upset her or the fact that it will do so.

The result is that Ellen's epistemically insincere testimony fails to make epistemic grounds available to transmit to Sarah. Moreover, we can see that can be generalised to the conclusion that epistemically insincere testimony does not make epistemic grounds available to transmit. Making epistemic grounds available to transmit by testimony involves putting the listener in a position to form a belief based on those epistemic grounds by believing the speaker's testimony. Where the speaker's testimony is epistemically insincere, the speaker's testimony is not connected to any epistemic grounds in the right way and thus does not make epistemic grounds available to transmit.

We should therefore doubt Faulkner's claim that a speaker's testimony can make epistemic grounds available to transmit even if it is not epistemically sincere. A speaker's testimony being epistemically sincere is a necessary condition of her testimony making epistemic grounds available to transmit. It is equally easy to see why the speaker's testimony being epistemically sincere is a sufficient condition of her testimony making epistemic grounds available to transmit. In a case where the speaker's testimony is epistemically sincere, the reason why she says that ϕ is the fact that someone's epistemic grounds are epistemic grounds for ϕ. There is thus an important connection between the transmitted epistemic grounds and the speaker's testimony. The result is that, if the listener believes the speaker when she says that ϕ, the listener's belief can be connected to someone's epistemic grounds for ϕ in the way required for basing.

Suppose that Anna tells Lydia that the Eiffel Tower is 324 metres tall and her testimony, when she does so, is epistemically sincere. It follows from this that the reason why Anna said that the Eiffel Tower is 324 metres tall is the fact that someone's (possibly her own) epistemic grounds are epistemic grounds for thinking that the Eiffel Tower is 324 metres tall, and it follows from this that this is, in an important way, why she says it. In terms of the epistemic basing relation, the fact that there is this kind of connection to the epistemic grounds means that, if a listener forms her belief that the Eiffel Tower is 324 metres tall on the basis of the speaker's testimony, her belief can be based on the epistemic grounds that feature in the explanation of why the speaker said this.

Those who endorse transmission in the strong sense should thus maintain that a speaker's testimony making epistemic grounds available to transmit is a matter of the speaker's testimony being epistemically sincere, where epistemic sincerity is a matter of the reason why the speaker says that ϕ being the fact that someone's epistemic grounds are epistemic grounds for ϕ. In a situation where this is the case, the speaker's testimony can put a listener in a position to believe that ϕ on the basis of the epistemic grounds that are the reason why the speaker said that ϕ. In a situation where this is not the case, however, the speaker's testimony cannot do this.

2.4   The availability of knowledge

With an account of the conditions under which a speaker's testimony makes epistemic grounds available to transmit, we can turn to the question of when a speaker's testimony makes knowledge available to transmit. The account of the conditions under which a speaker's testimony makes epistemic grounds available to transmit as given in **(TG-N)**, combined with the account of knowledge transmission as given in **(TK)**, gives rise to the following claim:

(TK-N)   A speaker's testimony that ϕ makes knowledge that ϕ available to transmit if and only if the speaker's testimony that ϕ makes epistemic grounds for ϕ available to transmit from someone who knows that ϕ.

As with the statements about what the transmission of knowledge and epistemic grounds involve – given in **(TK)** and **(TG)** respectively – the statements in **(TK-N)** and **(TG-N)** respect the thought that the transmission of epistemic grounds is the fundamental notion both conceptually and epistemically.

Equally, the statement in **(TK-N)** allows that knowledge can be transmitted in a case where there is no knowledge in the testimonial chain, but not in a case where there is no knowledge *simpliciter*.[18] Moreover, the claim that a speaker's testimony making epistemic grounds available to transmit is a necessary condition of the speaker's testimony making knowledge available to transmit, plus the claim that a speaker's testimony being epistemically sincere is a necessary condition of the speaker's testimony making epistemic grounds available to transmit – as **(TG-N)** states – entails that the speaker's testimony being epistemically sincere is a necessary condition of the speaker's testimony making knowledge available to transmit.

What, then, are the alternatives to **(TK-N)**? Elizabeth Fricker (2015) offers one account. Rather than suggesting that a speaker's testimony that ϕ makes knowledge that ϕ available to transmit if and only if it makes epistemic grounds for ϕ available to transmit from someone who knows that ϕ, Fricker suggests that a speaker's testimony makes knowledge available to transmit if and only if the speaker is such that not easily would she assert that ϕ unless she knew that ϕ (Fricker 2015, p. 187). Fricker's theory is a transmission theory in the moderate sense of transmission, but the comparison is nevertheless useful.

Rather than focusing on the reason why the speaker said that ϕ, Fricker's account focuses on how easily the speaker might have asserted that φ without knowing that φ. Insofar as the closest possible world in which the speaker asserts that φ but does not know that φ is further away, the speaker is such that not easily would she assert that φ unless she knew that φ. In other words, according to Fricker's account, what matters is the *safety* of the fact that the speaker knows that φ, given the fact that she asserts that φ.

To compare the view in (**TK-N**) with the view that Fricker proposes, we might consider two cases. In one, the speaker's testimony is epistemically sincere but the speaker is not such that not easily would she assert that φ unless she knew that φ. In the other, the speaker is such that not easily would she assert that φ unless she knew that φ, but her testimony is not epistemically sincere. Both cases, I believe, favour the view given in (**TK-N**).

Consider a case in which Laura tells Emily that the soup that they are preparing needs more salt. The reason why she does this is that she tasted the soup and was able to tell that the soup needs more salt, bringing her to know this. She has some epistemic grounds for thinking that the soup needs more salt, and this is why she tells Emily this. Unbeknownst to either Laura or Emily, however, they are being watched by Chloe, and if Laura had not been about to tell Emily that the soup needed more salt, Chloe would have intervened to make her do so.[19]

In this situation, it is clear that Laura's testimony is epistemically sincere. The reason why she tells Emily that the soup needs more salt is that her epistemic grounds are epistemic grounds for thinking that this is the case. Equally, however, Laura is not such that not easily would she assert that the soup needed more salt unless she knew this to be the case. If she did not know this to be the case, then it is true that she would not have been disposed to assert that the soup needed more salt. But Chloe's disposition to intervene means that she would nonetheless have asserted this. Laura would not have asserted this in the same way that she actually does, but she would have asserted it nonetheless.[20]

Does Laura's testimony make knowledge available to transmit in this case? I think it does. The fact that Chloe does nothing means that what actually happens in this situation is a straightforward case of someone telling a listener something that she knows. Laura says that the soup needs more salt, and the reason why she does this is the fact that her epistemic grounds are epistemic grounds for thinking that this is the case. If Emily believes her, then her belief that the soup needs more salt can be connected to Laura's epistemic grounds for this in the way associated with transmission. Since Emily's epistemic grounds are good enough to provide her with the kind of access to the fact required for knowledge, her testimony can put Laura in a similar position and thus make knowledge available to transmit.

The fact that the closest possible world in which Laura does not have epistemic grounds for this is one in which she says it anyway means that her testimony does not make knowledge available to transmit to Emily in that world. But we should not move from the observation that Laura's testimony does not make knowledge available to transmit to Emily in *that* world to the observation that it does not in the *actual* world. In the actual world, Laura's testimony is connected to the epistemic grounds that ground her knowledge that the soup needs more salt, and her testimony thus makes knowledge available to transmit to Emily.

Testimony can therefore make knowledge available to transmit in cases where the speaker's testimony is epistemically sincere, even if the speaker is not such that not easily would she assert what she does unless she knew it. What matters in such cases is the fact that the speaker's testimony is nonetheless epistemically sincere. What about the reverse case? Can testimony make knowledge available to transmit in a situation where the speaker is such that not easily would she assert what she does unless she knew it, but the speaker's testimony is not epistemically sincere?

I believe that it cannot. Suppose that Johanna tells Rachel that the time is 11:15. She knows that it is 11:15, but this is nothing to do with the reason why she tells Rachel this. Rather, she tells Rachel that the time is 11:15 because she knows that Rachel has a meeting at midday and Johanna wants to reassure her that she has plenty of time. Unbeknownst to either Johanna or Rachel, however, Johanna is being observed by Lucy and, if Johanna had been disposed to assert something that she did not know, Lucy would have intervened to stop her. As it happens, Johanna knows what she says and Lucy does nothing.

In this case, Johanna's testimony is not epistemically sincere. But assuming that Lucy is sufficiently skilled at intervening, she is such that not easily would she assert what she does unless she knew it. The fact that it is 11:15, the fact that Johanna knows that it is 11:15 and the fact that Johanna has epistemic grounds for thinking that it is 11:15 have nothing to do with the reason why she asserts this. The reason why she asserts it is either that she believes that it will reassure Rachel that she has plenty of time before her meeting or, if she knows this, the fact that it will reassure Rachel that she has plenty of time before her meeting.

Johanna's testimony thus does not make knowledge available to transmit to Rachel. The fact that Johanna's testimony has nothing to do with the fact that the time is 11:15, or her epistemic grounds, or her knowledge, means that believing her testimony cannot cause Rachel to be related to the fact that it is 11:15 in the way required for her to know. If she subsequently relaxes and stops rushing around, the reason for this might be that she believes that the time is 11:15, or it might be that Johanna told her that the time is 11:15, but, intuitively, it is not the fact that it is 11:15. The fact that it is 11:15 cannot be the reason why she stops rushing around, and the reason for this is that she does not know it. As a result, Johanna's testimony does not make knowledge available to transmit.

We have thus seen that, in cases where the account in **(TK-N)** and Fricker's account of when testimony makes knowledge available to transmit come apart, the account in **(TK-N)** provides an intuitively adequate characterisation.

2.5 Conclusion

I have been arguing for the following principles concerning the conditions under which testimony makes knowledge and epistemic grounds available to transmit:

(TG-N) A speaker's testimony that ϕ can make epistemic grounds for ϕ available to transmit to a listener if and only if the speaker's testimony that ϕ is epistemically sincere.

(TK-N) A speaker's testimony that ϕ makes knowledge that ϕ available to transmit if and only if the speaker's testimony that ϕ makes epistemic grounds for ϕ available to transmit from someone who knows that ϕ.

Three further points are worth emphasising. First, the examples of epistemic sincerity have primarily been focused on cases in which the speaker deliberates and decides what to say. However, this is not a necessary condition of epistemic sincerity. A speaker's testimony that ϕ might be epistemically sincere because she has epistemic grounds for ϕ and the possibility of saying something other than what her epistemic grounds best support does not enter her head. The reason why such a speaker says that ϕ might nonetheless be the fact that her epistemic grounds are epistemic grounds for ϕ.

Second, the conception of epistemic sincerity is compatible with someone making knowledge and epistemic grounds for ϕ available to transmit via a speech act other than an assertion that ϕ. A junior committee member, upon recognising that the strategy being discussed is the same as the one discussed at the previous meeting, might timidly ask *is this strategy similar to the one discussed at the previous meeting?* Insofar as the reason why she does so might be the fact that her epistemic grounds are epistemic grounds for thinking that this is the case, her speech act might make knowledge and epistemic grounds available to transmit to someone who reinterpreted her question as a statement.

Third, note that the statements in **(TG-N)** and **(TK-N)** are not intended to account for the availability of *all* knowledge and epistemic grounds made available by testimony. Rather, they are intended to account for when knowledge and epistemic grounds are made available to transmit. It might well be that a listener can come to know something on the basis of a speaker's testimony in a case where the speaker's testimony is not epistemically sincere. But this knowledge cannot be explained in terms of transmission.

Notes

1 In this spirit, John McDowell (1994) states that:

> The idea of knowledge by testimony is that if a knower gives intelligible expression to his knowledge, he puts it into the public domain, where it can be picked up by those who can understand the expression, as long as the opportunity is not closed to them because it would be doxastically irresponsible to believe the speaker (McDowell 1994, p. 438).

2 Advocates of **(TG-N$_1$)** include Robert Audi (2006), John McDowell (1994) and David Owens (2000). Some argue for **(TG-N$_1$)** independently of a commitment to endorsing transmission in the strong sense; others connect the two.

3 Advocates of **(TG-N$_2$)** include Tyler Burge (1993), Paul Faulkner (2011) and Elizabeth Fricker (2006). Again, not all of these discussions endorse transmission in the strong sense, but all endorse **(TG-N$_2$)**.

4 Jennifer Lackey (2008) and J. Adam Carter & Philip J. Nickel (2014) discuss cases of this type.

5 On this sense of sincerity, see Allan Gibbard (1994), Edward Hinchman (2013), David Owens (2006) and Mike Ridge (2005).

6 This account of epistemic sincerity is developed from the account given in Stephen Wright (2016).

7 Again, though I am sympathetic to it, nothing that follows presupposes or depends on the truth of Hyman's view.

8 John McDowell's (1994) discussion of testimony exploits a similar distinction, between cases in which a listener comes to know what a speaker says and thus has access to the factive reason *that she heard from the speaker that φ*, rather than merely *that she heard the speaker say that φ* (McDowell 1994, p. 210).

9 Hyman calls these 'grounds', but to avoid confusion with epistemic grounds, I shall use the term 'motivation'.

10 Hyman (2015) discusses this in much more detail. See Chapter 6 in particular.

11 The idea that someone who knows that φ is able to do something in such a way that the fact that φ is the reason why she does it is not unique to theories that take knowledge to be an ability. See, for example, Tim Williamson (2000) and Kieran Setiya (2013).

12 As we have previously observed, there might be content that cannot be known on the basis of testimony, such as content concerning moral or aesthetic matters. Something similar might be true of *de se* knowledge. Such cases are intended to be outside the scope of **(TG-N)**.

13 By this I do not mean to imply that a speaker's testimony that φ is epistemically sincere only if φ is true, or that one can have epistemic grounds for φ only if φ is true. The conception of epistemic sincerity is adequate even if φ is possible.

14 For surveys of the literature, see Korcz (1997, 2002).

15 Classic examples of causal approaches to the epistemic basing relation come from Donald Davidson (1980) and Alvin Plantinga (1993). For more recent treatments, see Tom Kelly (2002) and John Turri (2011).

16 See Marshall Swain (1979).

17 See Ian Evans (2013).

18 Cf. Burge's (1993) claim that 'knowledge of a simple logical truth does not depend on anything further than understanding and believing it, whereas knowledge based on interlocution depends on there being knowledge in the chain of sources beyond the recipient' (Burge 1993, p. 480, n. 19).

19 Chloe's intervention is thus similar to that found in Frankfurt cases. See Harry Frankfurt (1969) and Kadri Vihvelin (2000). Sanford Goldberg (2005) also uses the idea of *silent monitoring* in a case where an intervener would intervene to correct a speaker if she were to say something false. We shall return to Goldberg's case in §7.4.

20 One might worry that the fact that Chloe forces her to say that the soup needs more salt in the worlds where Laura is not disposed to say this means that her testimony cannot qualify as an assertion. This, I believe, is a mistake. David Owens (2006) gives examples of statements that are not freely made – for example, those made under hypnosis – but still nonetheless qualify as assertions.

Bibliography

Audi, R. (2006). Testimony, credulity, and veracity. In J. Lackey and E. Sosa (Eds.), *The Epistemology of Testimony*, pp. 25–49. Oxford: Oxford University Press.

Burge, T. (1993). Content preservation. *Philosophical Review* 102(4), 457–488.

Carter, J. A. and P. J. Nickel (2014). On testimony and transmission. *Episteme* 11(2), 145–155.

Davidson, D. (1980). *Essays on Actions and Essays on Actions and Events*. Oxford: Oxford University Press.

Evans, I. (2013). The problem of the basing relation. *Synthese* 190(14), 2943–2957.

Faulkner, P. (2011). *Knowledge on Trust*. Oxford: Oxford University Press.

Frankfurt, H. (1969). Alternate possibilities and moral responsibility. *Journal of Philosophy* 66(23), 829–839.

Fricker, E. (2006). Second-hand knowledge. *Philosophy and Phenomenological Research* 73(3), 592–618.

Fricker, E. (2015). How to make invidious distinctions amongst reliable testifiers. *Episteme* 12(2), 173–202.

Gibbard, A. (1994). *Wise Choices, Apt Feelings*. Oxford: Oxford University Press.

Goldberg, S. (2005). Testimonial knowledge through unsafe testimony. *Analysis* 65(288), 302–311.

Hinchman, E. (2013). Assertion, sincerity, and knowledge. *Noûs* 47(4), 613–646.

Hyman, J. (2015). *Action, Knowledge, and Will*. Oxford: Oxford University Press.

Kelly, T. (2002). The rationality of belief and some other propositional attitudes. *Philosophical Studies* 110(2), 163–196.

Korcz, K. (1997). Recent work on the basing relation. *American Philosophical Quarterly* 34(2), 171–192.

Korcz, K. (2000). The causal doxastic theory of the basing relation. *Canadian Journal of Philosophy* 30(4), 525–550.

Lackey, J. (2008). *Learning from Words: Testimony as a Source of Knowledge.* Oxford: Oxford University Press.

McDowell, J. (1994). Knowledge by hearsay. In B. Matilal and A. Chakrabarti (Eds.), *Knowing from Words*, pp. 195–224. Dordrecht: Kluwer Academic Publishers.

Owens, D. (2000). *Reason Without Freedom: The Problem of Epistemic Normativity.* London: Routledge.

Owens, D. (2006). Testimony and assertion. *Philosophical Studies* 130(1), 105–129.

Plantinga, A. (1993). *Warrant: The Current Debate.* Oxford: Oxford University Press.

Ridge, M. (2005). Sincerity and expressivism. *Philosophical Studies* 131(2), 487–510.

Setiya, K. (2013). Causality in action. *Analysis* 73(3), 501–512.

Swain, M. (1979). Justification and the basis of belief. In G. Pappas (Ed.), *Justification and Knowledge*, pp. 25–50. Dordrecht: D. Reidel Publishing Company.

Turri, J. (2011). Believing for a reason. *Erkenntnis* 74(3), 383–397.

Vihvelin (2000). Freedom, foreknowledge, and the principle of alternate possibilities. *Canadian Journal of Philosophy* 30(1), 1–23.

Williamson, T. (2000). *Knowledge and its Limits.* Oxford: Oxford University Press.

Wright, S. (2016). Sincerity and transmission. *Ratio* 29(1), 42–56.

3 Acquisition

3.1 Introduction

Having seen the conditions under which a speaker's testimony makes knowledge and epistemic grounds available to transmit, we can turn to the question of when such knowledge and epistemic grounds are acquired by a listener. This time, we can take the question of knowledge and the question of epistemic grounds together.

A listener acquiring knowledge that ϕ and epistemic grounds for ϕ through transmission typically involves the listener believing the speaker's testimony that ϕ. As we shall see in Chapter 6, it also depends on the listener coming to believe a speaker's testimony in a particular way. This chapter, however, will be concerned with a more general preliminary question. It is obvious that a listener cannot acquire knowledge and epistemic grounds through transmission if she is aware of reasons *against* believing the speaker's testimony. This is because these considerations would *defeat* her acquisition of knowledge and epistemic grounds. Our question here, then, concerns whether a listener acquiring knowledge that ϕ or epistemic grounds *for* ϕ through transmission depends on the listener being aware of reasons for believing the speaker's testimony?

There are two views available on the subject of epistemic grounds:

(TG-S$_1$) A listener can acquire epistemic grounds for ϕ through transmission only if the listener is aware of reasons for believing the speaker's testimony that ϕ.

(TG-S$_2$) A listener can acquire epistemic grounds for ϕ through transmission even if the listener is not aware of reasons for believing the speaker's testimony that ϕ.

(TG-S$_2$) is the orthodox view.[1] Of course, those who endorse (TG-S$_2$) also insist that a listener cannot acquire epistemic grounds through transmission if she is aware of reasons *against* believing the speaker's testimony.

We shall return to this issue in §3.4. For now, though, the central point is that those who maintain **(TG-S₂)** claim that a listener can acquire epistemic grounds made available to transmit even without being aware of reasons for believing the speaker's testimony.

I shall argue that transmission theorists ought to endorse **(TG-S₂)**. The argument takes the form of a dilemma for advocates of **(TG-S₁)**. Transmission theorists who endorse **(TG-S₁)** must either endorse or deny the claim that the listener's reasons for believing the speaker's testimony are the reason why she believes what the speaker says, but either option is problematic. Since no such dilemma arises for transmission theorists who endorse **(TG-S₂)**, I conclude that transmission theorists should endorse **(TG-S₂)**.

3.2 Testimony and rationality

The dispute over **(TG-S₁)** and **(TG-S₂)** is an internal dispute among transmission theorists. But the considerations in support of them are of wider significance. The argument that I shall make applies not only to transmission theories but also to any theory of testimony that seeks to maintain that a listener acquiring epistemic grounds through testimony depends on her being aware of reasons for believing the speaker's testimony, but that listener's epistemic grounds extend beyond these reasons. These theories are *dualist* theories. Transmission theories that endorse **(TG-S₁)** are one such type of theory, but there are others. Most notably, there is the approach to testimony advocated by Jennifer Lackey.[2] The objection to **(TG-S₁)** here is thus an objection to dualist approaches in general, which is applied specifically to the question of transmission.

What is there to be said for **(TG-S₁)** and **(TG-S₂)** respectively? More generally, what is there to be said for or against the idea that a listener having epistemic grounds for what a speaker says depends on her being aware of reasons for believing the speaker's testimony? Traditionally, motivations have been organised around the issues of gullibility and scepticism. Those who endorse **(TG-S₁)** – or, more generally, maintain that the acquisition of epistemic grounds depends on the listener being aware of reasons for believing the speaker's testimony – have tended to argue that denying this claim leads to the unintuitive claim that someone can acquire epistemic grounds by being gullible.

By contrast, those who endorse **(TG-S₂)** – or the claim that a listener's acquisition of epistemic grounds from testimony does not depend on her being aware of reasons for believing the speaker's testimony – maintain that denying this claim makes epistemic grounds from testimony implausibly difficult to come by. The result thus seems to be something of a familiar balancing act. On the one hand, epistemic grounds from testimony must not be too easy to come by. Providing an epistemic charter for the gullible and the undiscriminating, in Elizabeth Fricker's famous words, is problematic, but so too is a sceptical epistemology of testimony.[3]

The general idea behind arguments for **(TG-S₂)** and related principles is summarised in the opening of Leslie Stevenson's (1993) discussion of testimony:

> Very often, the only answer one can give to the question 'How do you know?' is 'Someone told me so'. [. . .] If we were not entitled thus to rely on testimony, each of us would know very much less than we think we do – only what one has seen for oneself, or what one can inductively support or deductively prove with one's unaided resources. With some claims one might, if one took enough trouble, check the matter out for oneself, and justify one's judgement by perception or proof. But in many other cases – such as assertions about the past, about present events too far away to be perceived, or about matters beyond one's scientific or mathematical competence – verification by the hearer is out of the question.
>
> (Stevenson 1993, p. 429)

An initial motivation for **(TG-S₂)** comes from the observation that we do not ordinarily take our epistemic grounds from other sources to depend on our being aware of reasons for believing the deliverances of those sources. This point is made in the literature with respect to perception, memory and instruments.[4] Since the epistemic grounds that we get from these sources do not depend on us being aware of reasons for believing the deliverances that they yield, why should anything different be true of testimony?

Furthermore, those who endorse principles in the spirit of **(TG-S₂)** are also apt to maintain that the idea that our epistemic grounds from testimony do depend on us being aware of reasons for believing what speakers say quickly leads to a sceptical epistemology of testimony.[5] Recently, this idea has gained some additional momentum from the evidence from social psychology, which indicates that listeners are typically not sensitive to signs of truth and falsity when they are told things by speakers.[6] We shall return to the evidence from social psychology in §4.3. For our present purposes, though, it is important to note that advocates of **(TG-S₂)** might appeal to the evidence from social psychology to show that the acquisition of epistemic grounds through testimony does not depend on the listener being aware of reasons for thinking that the speaker's testimony is true.

In a similar spirit, advocates of principles like **(TG-S₂)** appeal to the idea that children and infants can come to acquire epistemic grounds by believing what they are told. Even if there is disagreement over the question of whether or not adults are aware of reasons in cases where they acquire epistemic grounds through testimony, it surely seems plausible that children come to acquire epistemic grounds without being aware of reasons for believing what they are told.[7] Again, the idea is that avoiding a sceptical epistemology of testimony depends on allowing that listeners can come to acquire epistemic grounds without being aware of reasons for believing what speakers say.

This last-mentioned consideration does not strike me as a particularly strong one. Interestingly, though, even those who reject **(TG-S$_2$)** take the observations about children to have intuitive force. For example, Lackey, who rejects transmission altogether but endorses an analogue of **(TG-S$_1$)**, and Faulkner, who endorses **(TG-S$_1$)**, both argue that children typically have more sophistication than advocates of this type of argument allow, and the claim that they are able to acquire epistemic grounds through testimony does not impugn **(TG-S$_1$)** or analogous claims. Likewise, Fricker, who makes some of the most forceful arguments concerning gullibility, allows that a listener being aware of reasons for believing a speaker's testimony is not a necessary condition of her acquiring epistemic grounds in the case of children as listeners.[8]

For my own part, whilst I am sympathetic to **(TG-S$_2$)**, I am doubtful about the force of the observation that children are not sensitive to reasons when they consider what they are told. If a critic of **(TG-S$_2$)** claimed that children do not acquire epistemic grounds at the time that they are told things, she might still claim that they come to acquire epistemic grounds when they subsequently become aware of such reasons and become sensitive to them.[9] The intuition that children do not acquire epistemic grounds for what they are told at the time that they receive testimony – and it is crucial that the intuition is that children acquire epistemic grounds *at the time that they are told* – does not strike me as non-negotiable. Others, however, seem to disagree.

On the other side of the disagreement, there are considerations in favour of the idea that a listener acquiring epistemic grounds through testimony depends on the listener being aware of reasons for believing the speaker's testimony. Where some argue that, as far as other epistemic sources are concerned, our beliefs are supported by epistemic grounds even if we are not aware of reasons for believing their deliverances, others maintain that this is not, in fact, true. Insofar as someone is genuinely not aware of reasons for believing on the basis of an epistemic source, that epistemic source does not provide her with epistemic grounds.[10]

Equally, one might maintain **(TG-S$_1$)** on the basis of considerations that are distinctive to testimony. One might think that, regardless of what we should think of other epistemic sources, there are considerations that are distinctive to testimony that, by themselves, establish the claim that a listener acquiring epistemic grounds from testimony depends on her being aware of reasons for believing the speaker's testimony. Lackey argues for a principle analogous to **(TG-S$_1$)** based on the intuitive claim that believing what the speaker says without being aware of reasons for doing so is irrational. Lackey's case involves someone who seems to see an alien drop a diary and, without being aware of reasons for doing so, believes what appears to be written in it. Lackey maintains that the subject's belief in this case is sufficiently irrational for it to be incompatible with her acquiring epistemic grounds in this way (Lackey 2008, pp. 168–169).

Various objections have been placed against this idea. One line of response suggests that the case is sufficiently difficult to imagine, which renders it unclear as to what our intuitions about this kind of case ought to be. In a case where the listener *really* has no reasons for or against believing on the basis of the apparent diary, it is far from clear that the listener really is irrational in believing what the diary appears to say.[11] Furthermore, if we do manage to theorise accurately about the case, then the intuition that the listener is irrational might be underpinned by the idea that the listener is actually aware of reasons against believing in this way.[12]

In a similar spirit, Faulkner develops the Argument from Cooperation. This begins with the observation that speakers and listeners enter into conversations with distinctive practical interests. Listeners want to believe truths; speakers want to influence listeners by being believed. More generally, speakers want to be believed regardless of whether or not they are telling the truth, whereas listeners want to believe what speakers say only if they are telling the truth. There is therefore, by default, a conflict of interests between speakers and listeners in testimonial situations. The listener can recognise the speaker's interests and know that they conflict with her own. The result is that believing what a speaker says without being aware of reasons for doing is irrational and thus incompatible with the acquisition of epistemic grounds (Faulkner 2011, p. 7).

Of course, a listener's interests and a speaker's interests might align in any given case. There are clearly cases in which a speaker and a listener both have an interest in having the listener believe something true. However, this is not the point of the Argument from Cooperation. The point is that there is a conflict of interests in *general* terms, which can be put in game theoretic terms. The outcome that is best for the speaker is the one in which she tells the truth in certain situations and not in others, but the listener believes in all of them. The best outcome for the listener is one in which the speaker always tells the truth and the listener believes what she says only if she does so. These general interests thus generate a conflict between the speaker's best outcome and the listener's best outcome.

Weighing these competing considerations against each other is extremely difficult. It may even be that there is no single correct way to do this. It might be that one person can find the motivations for **(TG-S₁)** more compelling, whilst someone else finds the motivations for **(TG-S₂)** more compelling, without either of them somehow misjudging the evidence.[13] Fortunately, I believe that resolving the dispute over which principle transmission theorists should adopt does not require us to weigh these considerations against each other.

The existing dispute between advocates of **(TG-S₁)** and **(TG-S₂)** has typically operated on the assumption that transmission theorists are at liberty to choose between the two principles on the basis of whatever reasons they find compelling. In other words, nothing in the definition of transmission brings with it any commitment to endorsing **(TG-S₁)** over **(TG-S₂)**, or vice versa. The idea is that the question of which principle concerning the acquisition of epistemic grounds through testimony is correct is independent of the issue of what transmission involves. This, however, is mistaken. Those who endorse transmission should endorse **(TG-S₂)** over **(TG-S₁)** simply in virtue of being transmission theorists.

3.3   The first horn of the dilemma

The argument for this takes the form of a dilemma for those who endorse **(TG-S₁)**. The argument can be summarised as follows:

(5) Transmission theorists who endorse **(TG-S₁)** must either endorse or deny the claim that a listener can acquire knowledge and epistemic grounds through transmission only if the reason why the listener believes what the speaker says is the fact that she has reasons for doing so.

(6) If the claim is true, then the acquisition of knowledge and epistemic grounds through transmission is impossible.

(7) If the claim is false, then the claim that a listener's acquisition of knowledge and epistemic grounds through transmission depends on her being aware of reasons for believing the speaker's testimony – expressed in **(TG-S₁)** – is false.

Therefore

(8) The claim in **(TG-S₁)** is not compatible with the claim that testimony transmits knowledge and epistemic grounds.

In light of this, transmission theorists should endorse **(TG-S₂)**, rather than **(TG-S₁)**. I shall take **(5)** as given. In this section, I shall argue for the claim in **(6)**. In the following section, I shall argue for the claim in **(7)**. In concluding, I shall show why no version of this dilemma can be used to argue against **(TG-S₂)**.

The argument for **(6)** rests on a pair of cases. The first is from Lackey. In Lackey's case, a listener has an unerring ability to distinguish between true and false statements. When the listener hears a true statement, her left temple throbs and she believes what the speaker says. When the listener hears a false statement, her right temple throbs and she identifies the statement as false. Over time, she has come to acquire good reasons for thinking that she has this capacity. One day, a speaker who generally says false things actually says something true. The listener recognises her statement as true and believes what she says (Lackey 2008, pp. 90–91).

In this case, the reason why the listener believes what the speaker says is the fact that she has reasons for doing so. As Lackey notes, however, the speaker's testimony has nothing to do with the listener's epistemic grounds. As Lackey puts it, 'the testimony itself simply drops out of the epistemic picture' (Lackey 2008, p. 91). The idea is that the epistemic grounds that support the listener's belief are simply a matter of the reasons that she uses in believing. Since the reason why she believes is the fact that she has reasons for thinking that the speaker's testimony is true, the epistemic grounds that support her belief do not extend beyond these reasons.

This is not to say that the listener cannot come to know what the speaker says in this way. It is, however, to say that the listener cannot acquire knowledge or epistemic grounds *through transmission* in this way. In order for her belief to be supported by transmitted epistemic grounds – a necessary condition of her acquiring knowledge through transmission – the reason why the listener believes is the fact that the speaker says so. But a consequence of the listener believing in this way is that the reason why the listener believes is not the fact that the speaker says so, but the fact that the listener has reasons for thinking that the speaker's testimony is true.

Lackey agrees with this and claims that in such a case the speaker's testimony *causally triggers* the listener's belief, rather than causing it (Lackey 2008, p. 92). In the vocabulary of the epistemic basing relation, the listener's belief is not based on the speaker's testimony, and the result is that facts about the speaker's testimony – whether these are facts about it making knowledge and epistemic grounds available to transmit, or facts about it being reliably produced – are not relevant to the listener's belief.

Faulkner describes a similar case in which a maths teacher tells a student about a theorem and shows her the associated proof. Initially, the student does not understand the proof, but she believes the theorem nonetheless. Later, the student studies the proof and works through it for herself. In doing so, she comes to understand and appreciate the proof for herself.

In this case, the reason why the student believes the theorem changes from being the fact that the teacher said so to the fact that the student appreciates the proof. When the student believes the theorem but does not understand the proof, the reason why she believes the theorem is the fact that the teacher told her about it. Later, when she comes to understand the theorem for herself, the reason why she believes it is the fact that she understands the proof. In Faulkner's words, 'the student's belief, which is acquired by accepting the teacher's testimony, is testimonial at time t_1, but ceases to be testimonial at time t_2 once it is based on the proof' (Faulkner 2011, p. 18).

Faulkner's case and Lackey's case have an important similarity. They are both cases in which, intuitively, facts about the speaker's testimony – whether these are its reliability or its epistemic sincerity – are irrelevant in a case where the reason why the listener believes what the speaker says is the fact that the she has some reason for doing so. From these cases, we can develop a more general lesson, that in a case where the reason the listener believes what the speaker says is the fact that she has some reason for doing so, the epistemic grounds that support her belief do not extend beyond her reasons for believing the speaker's testimony.

Something similar comes up in Frederick F. Schmitt's (2006) discussion of the Transindividual Thesis. According to Schmitt, 'if my belief *p* is justified on testimony, then it is justified on the basis of the testifier's good reason to believe *p*, *unless on the basis of a good reason to believe p I myself possess*' (Schmitt 2006, p. 194, emphasis added). The idea is the same as the one that Lackey and Faulkner have expressed in terms of the basing relation. In a case where the listener's belief is based on her own reason, it is not based on the speaker's reasons. In other words, if the reason why the listener believes what the speaker says is the fact that she has reasons for doing so, the listener does not acquire transmitted knowledge or epistemic grounds.

Edward Hinchman (2014) also agrees with this point. According to Hinchman, when a speaker tells a listener something, she issues the listener with an invitation to trust the speaker not only for the truth of what she says, but with respect to the proposition that the speaker has adequate epistemic grounds for what she says to allow the listener to close her inquiries into it. However, if the listener does not take this then she fails to acquire the speaker's epistemic grounds for what she says. Hinchman states that 'assessing [a speaker] S for reliability is a way of refusing S's invitation to trust, since S is inviting A to trust her, not whatever evidence she thereby gives of her reliability' (Hinchman 2014, p. 17).

This is not to say that the listener taking the speaker's invitation to trust her is incompatible with her being aware of reasons for thinking that what the speaker says is true. A listener might well take a speaker's invitation when she is aware of reasons for thinking that the speaker's testimony is true. What matters, however, is that the listener's reasons for thinking that the speaker's testimony is true are not the reasons why she believes what the speaker says. A listener might happen to be aware of reasons for believing what a speaker says and nonetheless take up a speaker's invitation to trust her. But in this situation, the listener's awareness of reasons for believing what the speaker says is coincidental, rather than an explanatory factor in why the listener forms her belief.

Hinchman's explanation of why the reason that a listener believes a speaker's testimony being the fact that she is aware of reasons for doing so rules out the possibility of transmission is grounded in the interpersonal dynamics of the testimonial situation. On Hinchman's view, the interpersonal features of a testimonial situation are an important data point for the epistemology of testimony. The idea is that, in a case where the reason why the listener believes what the speaker says is the fact that she is aware of reasons for doing so, the listener does not believe what the speaker says in the way that the speaker intends for her to in telling her. Hinchman's idea is that the listener acting in this way fails to consummate the speech act and thus fails to acquire knowledge and epistemic grounds through transmission (Hinchman 2014, pp. 28–29).

There is, then, relatively wide support for the view that, in this type of case, the listener does not acquire knowledge and epistemic grounds made available to transmit by the speaker's testimony. This is because, in a case where the reason why the listener believes what the speaker says is the fact that she has reasons for doing so, it cannot also be the fact that the speaker said it. And it is only when the reason why the listener believes what the speaker says is the fact that the speaker said it that the listener acquires knowledge and epistemic grounds through transmission. This is the argument for **(6)**.

What could be said against this argument? An idea from Axel Gelfert (2014), whilst not directed explicitly at the argument here, might be thought to underpin one line of response. Gelfert's thought is that reasons for thinking that testimony is generally true might be used to licence a stance of taking testimony at face value unless there are reasons not to. The idea is that belief in testimony has two main stages. First, a listener uncovers reasons for thinking that testimony is generally true. Second, having done this, she decides on the basis of these reasons to believe what people say without reflecting further unless she is aware of reasons against doing so (Gelfert 2014, p. 140).

One might think that Gelfert's idea allows for the reason why the listener believes what the speaker says to be the fact that she has reasons for doing so in a way that does not undermine the idea that the listener also acquires knowledge and epistemic grounds through transmission when they are made available by a speaker's testimony. This, however, is too hasty. The reason that the listener is supposed to be able to acquire knowledge and epistemic grounds through transmission is that she does not believe by actively inferring what the speaker says when she says it. The concern, however, is not that the fact that the listener actively infers what the speaker says means that she does not acquire knowledge and epistemic grounds through transmission. Rather, the concern is that the fact that the listener is aware of reasons for believing what the speaker says is the reason why she does so means that her belief is not related to the speaker's knowledge and epistemic grounds in the way necessary for transmission.

Why does the listener forming her belief in this way entail that her belief is not related to the speaker's knowledge and epistemic grounds in the way necessary for transmission? A fact being the reason why someone believes something involves the subject being responsive to the fact in her believing. Also, a listener cannot be guided by both the fact that the speaker has epistemic grounds for what she says and the fact that she has reasons for believing what the speaker says. If one of the facts had been otherwise – if either the listener had been aware of reasons against believing what the speaker said, or if the speaker had lacked epistemic grounds for what she said – then the listener would have either believed or not believed, being guided by one fact or the other. And this is so even in a case where both facts point the listener in the direction of believing the speaker.

3.4   The second horn of the dilemma

The argument from the previous section shows that a listener can acquire available knowledge and epistemic grounds through transmission only if the reason why she believes what the speaker says is the fact that the speaker said it, rather than the fact that the listener is aware of such reasons. Transmission theorists who endorse (**TG-S$_1$**) must therefore maintain that a listener acquiring knowledge and epistemic grounds through transmission depends on her being aware of reasons for believing the speaker's testimony, but the fact that she is aware of such reasons must not be the reason why she believes what the speaker says. This view, however, is untenable, as I shall show in making the case for (**7**).

The trouble can be brought out by considering a further case. Suppose that someone is aware of various good reasons for thinking that the President of the USA is in Seattle. She reads this in a reputable newspaper, hears a friend saying that the President will be attending a concert at the Benaroya Hall later today and so on. Despite being aware of these reasons and despite being aware of no countervailing reasons, she refrains from forming the belief that the President is in Seattle until she consults her crystal ball and it tells her that the President is in Seattle. When the crystal ball tells her this, she comes to believe it.

Importantly, the idea is not that the crystal ball, in conjunction with the subject's other reasons, compels her to believe that the President is in Seattle. The idea is not that, whilst the subject's other reasons came up just short, the crystal tips her over the edge into believing. Rather, the idea is that the subject still does not regard her earlier reasons as compelling, but she regards the crystal ball's deliverance as a compelling reason by itself. The result is that the reason why she believes that the President is in Seattle is the fact that the crystal ball's deliverance said so.

Now, whatever one thinks about the rationality of the subject's belief in this case, it should be clear that the rationality of the subject's belief depends entirely on the rationality of believing on the basis of a crystal ball. One might think that the subject's belief is rational because beliefs held on the basis of the deliverances of a crystal ball are rational. One might think that it is irrational because beliefs held on the basis of the deliverances of a crystal ball are irrational. Or one might think that the question is not yet settled until further facts about the situation are stipulated. Whatever one thinks, the idea is that the rationality of the subject's belief stands or falls with the rationality of believing on the basis of a crystal ball.

The lesson that we should draw from this is that reasons that someone is aware of, but are not reasons why she believes something, do not contribute to the rationality of her belief. This means that, intuitively, there is no difference in terms of rationality between someone who believes that ϕ whilst being aware of reasons for doing so, but these are not the reason why she believes that ϕ, on the one hand, and someone who is not aware of reasons for believing that ϕ, on the other. This is important. It means that there is no difference in rationality between a listener who is aware of reasons for believing a speaker, but these are not why she believes what the speaker says, and a listener who is not aware of such reasons at all.

If there is no difference in rationality between these two listeners then it cannot be maintained that the listener being aware of such reasons is a necessary condition of a listener acquiring knowledge and epistemic grounds through transmission. Recall that the motivation for **(TG-S$_1$)** concerned rationality. If a listener who is aware of reasons for believing a speaker's testimony, but these are not the reason why the listener believes what the speaker says, is sufficiently rational to acquire knowledge and epistemic grounds through transmission, then so too is a listener who is not aware of such reasons.

This gives us the second horn of the dilemma. A transmission theorist who endorses **(TG-S₁)** cannot deny the claim that a listener acquiring knowledge and epistemic grounds through transmission depends on the reason why she believes what the speaker says being the fact that she is aware of reasons for doing so. The objection is not merely that this leaves **(TG-S₁)** unmotivated. If it merely showed that the view was unmotivated, then it might be salvaged by independent considerations. Rather, the objection shows that it is false. Intuitive considerations notwithstanding, maintaining **(TG-S₁)** in this way is problematic.

Taken together, the two horns of the dilemma make a case for **(TG-S₂)** over **(TG-S₁)**. What considerations might be brought to bear against **(TG-S₂)**? One objection is that a transmission theorist who endorses **(TG-S₂)** cannot simultaneously endorse the claim that a listener cannot acquire knowledge and epistemic grounds through transmission if she is aware of reasons against believing the speaker's testimony. This is an important claim and one that advocates of **(TG-S₂)** want to endorse. So, the observation that advocates of **(TG-S₂)** cannot endorse this claim in a principled way would amount to a substantial objection to **(TG-S₂)**.

Why might advocates of **(TG-S₂)** be unable to endorse the claim that a listener cannot acquire knowledge and epistemic grounds through transmission if she is aware of reasons against believing the speaker's testimony? One idea is that, once one accepts that a listener being aware of reasons against believing a speaker's testimony prevents her from acquiring knowledge and epistemic grounds through transmission, one is committed to accepting that a listener's acquisition of knowledge and epistemic grounds through transmission is a matter of rationality. And once one is committed to accepting that it is a matter of rationality, one is committed to accepting that a listener acquiring knowledge and epistemic grounds through transmission depends on her being aware of reasons for believing what the speaker says – contrary to **(TG-S₂)**.

The idea is that maintaining that a listener's acquisition of knowledge and epistemic grounds through transmission depends on her not being aware of reasons against believing the speaker's testimony, but not on her being aware of reasons for believing the speaker's testimony, is unprincipled. This, however, is mistaken. Robert Audi (1993) explains why. As Audi points out, if my garden is my source of food, then there are various things that I need for it to be the case in order for it to function as a food source. I am dependent on the sunshine, the rainfall, the ambient temperature and so on. Equally, I depend on people not poisoning the soil or animals eating my crops.

The fact that I depend on them not doing something, however, does not entail that I depend on them doing anything. The fact that they could interfere with my garden and thus scupper my food source does not make them part of my food source (Audi 1993, p. 144). In this situation, the fact that I depend on people not doing something does not entail that I depend on them doing something else. In the same way, the fact that a listener acquiring knowledge and epistemic grounds through transmission depends on the listener not being aware of reasons against believing what the speaker says does not entail that the listener acquiring knowledge and epistemic grounds through transmission depends on the listener being aware of reasons for believing the speaker.[14]

3.4   Conclusion

I have been arguing that transmission theorists who endorse **(TG-S₁)** face a dilemma concerning whether or not the listener acquiring knowledge and epistemic grounds through transmission depends on the reason why she believes what the speaker says being the fact that she is aware of reasons for doing so. If this is true, then the acquisition of knowledge and epistemic grounds is impossible. If it is false, then **(TG-S₁)** is false.

No such dilemma arises for transmission theorists who defend **(TG-S₂)** and the analogous claim **(TK-S₂)**:

(TK-S₂)   A listener can acquire knowledge that φ through transmission even if the listener is not aware of reasons for believing the speaker's testimony that φ.

Such transmission theorists can straightforwardly maintain that a listener acquiring knowledge and epistemic grounds through transmission does not depend on the fact that she is aware of reasons for believing the speaker's testimony being the reason why she does so. Insofar as this entails that a listener can acquire knowledge and epistemic grounds through transmission without being aware of reasons for believing the speaker's testimony, this is entirely unproblematic as far as advocates of **(TG-S₂)** and **(TK-S₂)** are concerned.

More generally, whilst the dilemma does not arise for transmission theorists who defend **(TG-S₂)** and **(TK-S₂)**, it does arise for theorists who maintain that a listener's epistemic grounds extend beyond the reasons for believing the speaker's testimony that she is aware of, but that her belief being supported by such epistemic grounds depends on the reason why the listener believes what the speaker says being the fact that she is aware of such reasons. Transmission theorists who endorse **(TG-S₁)** are one example of such theorists, but others include the dualist approach advocated by Lackey.

Notes

1 Advocates of **(TG-S₂)** include Tyler Burge (1993, 1997), Edward Hinchman (2005, 2014), David Owens (2000) and Michael Welbourne (1986), amongst others. The main advocate of **(TG-S₁)** is Paul Faulkner (2011).
2 This kind of approach to testimony is plausibly also the result of applying the *anti-luck virtue epistemology* developed by Duncan Pritchard (2012) to the epistemology of testimony.
3 See Fricker (1994).
4 See James Pryor (2000) on perception, Tyler Burge (1993, 1997) on memory and Ernest Sosa (2010) on instruments.
5 This point is originally made by C.A.J Coady (1992, 1994).
6 See Joseph Shieber (2015) and Kourken Michaelian (2010).
7 Robert Audi (2013) is a prominent advocate of this argument.
8 See Lackey (2008), Faulkner (2011) and Fricker (1994).
9 Something like this is how Michaelian (2010) accounts for knowledge from testimony in response to the evidence from social psychology.
10 Classic discussions of this view are given by Laurence BonJour (1985) and Keith Lehrer (2000).
11 Martin Kusch (2013) makes this response.
12 This is Tim Perrine's (2014) response.
13 Peter van Inwagen (2010) takes the disagreement between himself and David Lewis regarding the compatibility of free will and determinism to be like this.
14 For more on why a listener being aware of reasons against φ prevents the fact that φ from being her reason for believing that φ, see Chapter 6 of John Hyman's (2015) discussion.

Bibliography

Audi, R. (1993). *The Structure of Justification*. Cambridge: Cambridge University Press.
Audi, R. (2013). Testimony as a social foundation of knowledge. *Philosophy and Phenomenological Research* 87(3), 507–531.
BonJour, L. (1985). *The Structure of Empirical Knowledge*. Cambridge, MA: Harvard University Press.
Burge, T. (1993). Content preservation. *Philosophical Review* 102(4), 457–488.
Burge, T. (1997). Interlocution, perception, and memory. *Philosophical Studies* 86(1), 21–47.
Coady, C. A. J. (1992). *Testimony: A Philosophical Study*. Oxford: Clarendon Press.
Coady, C. A. J. (1994). Testimony, observation and "autonomous knowledge". In B. Matilal and A. Chakrabarti (Eds.), *Knowing from Words*, pp. 225–250. Dordrecht: Kluwer Academic Publishers.
Faulkner, P. (2011). *Knowledge on Trust*. Oxford: Oxford University Press.

Fricker, E. (1994). Against gullibility. In B. Matilal and A. Chakrabarti (Eds.), *Knowing from Words*, pp. 125–161. Dordrecht: Kluwer Academic Publishers.

Gelfert, A. (2014). *A Critical Introduction to Testimony*. London: Bloomsbury.

Hinchman, E. (2005). Telling as inviting to trust. *Philosophy and Phenomenological Research* 70(3), 562–587.

Hinchman, E. (2014). Assurance and warrant. *Philosophers' Imprint* 14(17), 1–58.

Hyman, J. (2015). *Action, Knowledge, and Will*. Oxford: Oxford University Press.

Kusch, M. (2013). Jennifer Lackey on non-reductionism: A critique. In *Epistemology: Contexts, Values, Disagreement*, pp. 257–268. Berlin: De Gruyter.

Lackey, J. (2008). *Learning from Words: Testimony as a Source of Knowledge*. Oxford: Oxford University Press.

Lehrer, K. (2000). *Theory of Knowledge*, second edition. Boulder: Westview Press.

Michaelian, K. (2010). In defence of gullibility: The epistemology of testimony and the psychology of deception detection. *Synthese* 176(3), 399–427.

Owens, D. (2000). *Reason Without Freedom: The Problem of Epistemic Normativity*. London: Routledge.

Perrine, T. (2014). In defense of non-reductionism in the epistemology of testimony. *Synthese* 191(14), 3227–3237.

Pritchard, D. (2012). Anti-luck virtue epistemology. *Journal of Philosophy* 109(3), 247–279.

Pryor, J. (2000). The skeptic and the dogmatist. *Noûs* 34(4), 517–549.

Schmitt, F. F. (2006). Testimonial justification and transindividual reasons. In J. Lackey and E. Sosa (Eds.), *The Epistemology of Testimony*, pp. 193–224. Oxford: Oxford University Press.

Shieber, J. (2015). *Testimony: A Philosophical Introduction*. London: Routledge.

Sosa, E. (2010). *Knowing Full Well*. Princeton, NJ: Princeton University Press.

Stevenson, L. (1993). Why believe what people say? *Synthese* 94(3), 429–451.

Van Inwagen, P. (2010). We're right, they're wrong. In R. Feldman and T. Warfield (Eds.), *Disagreement*, pp. 10–28. Oxford: Oxford University Press.

Welbourne, M. (1986). *The Community of Knowledge*. Aberdeen, NJ: Aberdeen University Press.

4 Internalist approaches

4.1 Introduction

Thus far, we have seen the basic ideas behind transmission theories. We have seen what the transmission of knowledge and epistemic grounds involves and we have seen the conditions under which a speaker's testimony makes knowledge and epistemic grounds available to transmit. We have also seen that a listener can acquire knowledge and epistemic grounds through transmission, even if she is unaware of reasons for believing what the speaker says.

As yet, however, we have not seen any reason to think that the idea of transmission is important to the epistemology of testimony. This will be the focus of the remainder of the book. In this chapter and the next, I shall consider the prospects for theories that seek to account for testimony as an epistemic source without the idea of transmission. The first of these, which I shall consider here, is the internalist approach to the epistemology of testimony.

The internalist approach to the epistemology of testimony is the product of applying an internalist approach to epistemology more generally to the domain of testimony. Internalist approaches to epistemology in general are constituted by the endorsement of the following claim:

(I)   A subject's epistemic grounds for φ consist only in those reasons for φ that are internal to the subject.

Applied to the epistemology of testimony, this gives us the following claim:

(TI)   A listener's epistemic grounds for φ consist only in those reasons for believing a speaker's testimony that φ that are internal to the listener.

The statement in **(TI)** raises two important questions. The first concerns what it means to say that a reason is internal to a listener. The second concerns what kinds of reasons are internal to a listener. In the same way that, in discussing transmission, we distinguished between the question of what transmission involves and the question of under what conditions transmission takes place, we should distinguish between these two questions here.

Neither has a straightforward or uncontroversial answer. In response to the first, some maintain that a reason can be internal to a subject only if the reason is something that the subject is aware of, whereas others deny this. In response to the second, some maintain that factive reasons – those that are incompatible with the falsity of the subject's belief – can be internal to a subject, whereas others deny this. Let us begin by surveying both of these issues.

4.2   Internalism and the epistemology of testimony

We can bring out what it means for a reason to be internal to a listener by using two cases. In the first case, AJ is told by her friend that Johannes Kepler was born in 1571. AJ is aware of various reasons for thinking that her friend is a knowledgeable authority when it comes to historical scientific figures and also that her friend would not easily lie to her. AJ thus forms the belief that Kepler was born in 1571, and indeed her friend is both knowledgeable and epistemically sincere.

In the second case, AJ* is also told by her friend that Johannes Kepler was born in 1571. Like AJ in the first case, AJ* is aware of just as many and varied reasons for thinking that her friend is a knowledgeable authority when it comes to historical scientific figures and would not easily lie to her. AJ* thus forms the belief that Kepler was born in 1571. Unbeknownst to AJ*, however, her friend is not knowledgeable and epistemically sincere. Her statement is merely speculation, stated confidently in order to appear knowledgeable.

Now, are AJ and AJ* alike with respect to epistemic grounds? According to one version of internalism, they are. As far as they can tell, their experiences are indistinguishable, and the result is that their epistemic grounds are the same. Of course, they are not the same with respect to knowledge – presumably AJ's epistemic grounds put her in touch with the fact that Kepler died in 1571, whereas AJ*'s do not – but this difference in knowledge is not, according to this type of internalism, to be explained in terms of a difference in epistemic grounds. Quite simply, the fact that their experiences are subjectively indistinguishable entails that they are alike with respect to epistemic grounds.

This line of thinking is the product of applying the thoughts behind the New Evil Demon Argument to the epistemology of testimony.[1] The idea is that, when we consider these cases, or analogues of them, we should find it intuitive that the subjects are alike with respect to epistemic grounds. Theories that maintain that they are alike are *accessibilist* theories. So, considering these cases is supposed to make an argument for accessibilist approaches to epistemic grounds. Regardless of whether or not we find this argument convincing, we can use the cases to illustrate the idea behind accessibilist theories. According to accessibilist theories, if neither AJ nor AJ* can distinguish between the case of being told by someone who is knowledgeable and epistemically sincere and the case of being told by someone who is merely speculating, their epistemic grounds are the same.

The accessibilist idea is that the listeners are alike with respect to what they are aware of in virtue of the fact that they are unable to distinguish between the cases, and this means that they are alike with respect to epistemic grounds. Not all internalist theories accept this, though. Different internalist approaches reject different parts of the accessibilist view. Those who endorse mental-state internalism, or *mentalism*, maintain that AJ and AJ* are alike with respect to what they are aware of in virtue of being unable to distinguish between the cases but deny that this means that they are alike with respect to epistemic grounds.[2] On the other hand, *epistemological disjunctivist* approaches reject the claim that the listeners are alike with respect to what they are aware of in virtue of the fact that they are unable to distinguish between the cases.[3]

For the purposes of this discussion, we shall focus on accessibilist internalist theories. The reason for this is straightforward. It is only accessibilist approaches that constitute a genuine rival to transmission theories. If one takes a mental-state internalist or epistemological disjunctivist approach to the epistemology of testimony, then what emerges is a distinctive account of how transmission takes place, rather than a theory that maintains that it does not.[4]

The accessibilist approach thus gives us an idea of what it is for a reason to be internal to a listener. A reason is internal to a listener just in case it is something that she is aware of. The listener is aware of a reason just in case it is something that could be common between a case where the speaker is knowledgeable and epistemically sincere and a case where the speaker is not. But what reasons might a listener have for believing what a speaker says? There are three types of reasons: reasons for believing what people say generally, reasons for believing particular types of testimony and reasons for believing a particular instance of testimony.

One way in which a listener might come to believe what a speaker says is by reasoning as follows:

(9) Speaker S said that ϕ.
(10) People generally say true things.

Therefore

(11) ϕ.

When a listener believes what a speaker says in this way, the reason why she believes what the speaker says is the fact that she is aware of reasons for thinking that people generally say true things. As such, when a listener comes to know in this way, her knowledge is grounded in the reasons that she is aware of for thinking that people generally say true things. Traditionally, the idea that knowledge from testimony is grounded in reasons for thinking that people generally say true things that the listener is aware of is attributed to David Hume (1777).[5]

A corollary of the claim that knowledge from testimony is grounded in reasons that a listener is aware of for thinking that people generally say true things is that, if a listener is not aware of reasons for thinking that people generally say true things, then she does not come to know things by believing testimony. In other words, a listener coming to know things by believing testimony depends on her being aware of reasons for thinking that people generally say true things. This observation gives rise to the traditional objection to this view.

Intuitively, the idea that knowledge from testimony is grounded in reasons for thinking that people generally say true things is implausibly demanding. It seems that listeners can come to know things by believing testimony without having already established that people generally say true things. If this is correct, then the idea that knowledge from testimony is grounded in reasons for thinking that people generally say true things is false. It is worth noting that this traditional objection is advanced both by those who are sympathetic to internalist approaches to testimony, such as Elizabeth Fricker (1994, 1995), and those who are critical of it, such as C.A.J. Coady (1992, 1994).[6]

Rather than thinking that knowledge from testimony is grounded in reasons for thinking that people generally say true things, one might think that a listener can come to know what a speaker says by reasoning in the following way:

(12)   Speaker S said that ϕ in conditions C.
(13)   People who make assertions like ϕ in conditions C generally say true things.

Therefore

(14)   ϕ.[7]

This involves identifying a speaker's testimony as an instance of a specific type of testimony and then grounding knowledge from testimony in reasons for thinking that testimony of this type is generally true. Whilst this type of reasoning process no doubt can give rise to knowledge, appealing to *types* of testimony is not itself entirely uncontroversial. As Coady (1992) points out, in a case where someone produces testimony about a sick lion in Taronga Park Zoo, the statement is an instance of testimony about animals, testimony about what exists, testimony about medical matters and so on (Coady 1992, p. 84). Furthermore, it could be an instance of testimony from an adult, testimony from a medical expert, testimony from a friend and various other types.

Instances of testimony therefore belong to various different types. A listener's reasons for thinking that testimony of each of these types is generally true might be highly variable, though. A listener might have many good reasons for thinking that testimony about medical matters is generally true, but also reasons for thinking that testimony from the friend who produced it is generally false. Moreover, the problem of how to identify the testimony as an instance of one type of testimony rather than another is difficult to resolve. One might think, then, that there is more to the epistemology of testimony than reasons for thinking that people generally say true things and reasons for thinking that testimony of a particular type is generally true.

In light of these issues, internalist approaches typically maintain that knowledge from testimony is a matter of reasoning as follows:

(15) S said that φ.
(16) The fact that S said that φ indicates that φ.

Therefore

(17) φ.

Reasoning in this way does not involve implausible amounts of difficult background work on the part of the listener. She does not need to establish that people generally say true things or identify the speaker's testimony as an instance of testimony of a reliable type (though if she does succeed in either of these enterprises, she can still use this to ground her knowledge). Rather, the idea is that the listener simply needs to establish that the fact that the speaker said something on a particular occasion is best explained in terms of what she says being true.

How is a listener to establish this? The *locus classicus* of this idea is Fricker's (1994) discussion. According to Fricker, a listener 'should be continually evaluating [the speaker] for signs of trustworthiness throughout their exchange' (Fricker 1994, p. 151). Signs of insincerity, according to Fricker, are 'very frequently betrayed in a speaker's manner' (Fricker 1994, p. 150). Monitoring for competence involves considering the content of what the speaker says and reflecting on whether or not it is the kind of thing that is probably within the scope of the speaker's competences (Fricker 1994, p. 151). In doing so, the idea is that a speaker comes up with an account of why the speaker said what she did on the occasion in question. Insofar as the explanation features the truth of what the speaker says, it provides a reason for the listener to believe what the speaker says.[8]

This is the general idea behind internalist approaches to testimony. Internalist approaches maintain that a listener coming to know the truth of what the speaker says depends on the listener being aware of reasons for believing the speaker's testimony. However, they are not undermined by the dilemma that presents a problem for transmission theorists who endorse this claim. This is because internalist theories claim that a listener's epistemic grounds do not extend beyond the reasons that she uses in forming her belief. The result is that they can maintain that the listener's belief being supported by epistemic grounds does depend on the fact that she has reasons for doing so being the reason why she believes what the speaker says.

4.3   The evidence from social psychology

In this way, the idea of testimonial monitoring is important to internalist approaches. The reasons that ground knowledge from testimony, according to internalist approaches, are in turn grounded in the listener's monitoring of the speaker's testimony. One objection to internalist approaches is based on the idea that internalist theories typically overestimate the reliability of testimonial monitoring. According to this objection, the evidence from social psychology shows that listeners are generally not capable of distinguishing between true and false statements in a reliable way. The result is that internalist theories lead to an implausible scepticism about knowledge from testimony.

Kourken Michaelian (2010, 2013) and Joseph Shieber (2011, 2015) argue that the evidence from social psychology convincingly shows that testimonial monitoring does not enable listeners to distinguish between true and false statements in a reliable way. According to Michaelian,

> research in the psychology of deception detection – the term is used in the literature as a synonym of "lying" or "dishonesty" – implies that [. . .] monitoring is on a par (in terms both of the reliability of the process and of the sensitivity of the beliefs that it produces) with blind trust.
>
> (Michaelian 2010, p. 400)

Shieber makes a similar observation, stating that

> even a cursory reading of the social psychological literature that bears
> on the ways in which subjects form beliefs on the basis of testimony
> would seem to provide unimpeachably strong evidence that listeners
> cannot reliably distinguish between true and false statements.
>
> (Shieber 2015, p. 15)

The extent to which testimonial monitoring is unreliable is a source of divergence. Michaelian says that the average rate of accuracy for detecting deception is no higher than 57% (Michaelian 2010, p. 411). By contrast, Shieber states that accuracy rates have rarely risen above 60%, with some groups achieving accuracy rates of worse than 50% (Shieber 2015, p. 32). There is also disagreement as to exactly why testimonial monitoring is so unreliable. According to Michaelian, it is because listeners are not sufficiently sensitive to available signs (Michaelian 2010, p. 412). Shieber, however, maintains that the reason that testimonial monitoring is so unreliable is that the signs are simply not there to be picked up on (Shieber 2015, pp. 29–30).

Moreover, Michaelian and Shieber have differing views on the significance of the evidence from social psychology for internalist theories. Michaelian points out that the fact that beliefs do not amount to knowledge at the time that they are formed does not entail that they do not subsequently amount to knowledge. A listener might not be able to distinguish between true and false testimony at the time that she forms her belief, but it might nonetheless later become the case that, if her belief were not true, she would have found out about this, and the result is that she is subsequently in a position to know.[9] And Michaelian also argues that, whilst the evidence from social psychology shows that listeners are not typically able to distinguish between true and false statements at the time that they form their beliefs, they are subsequently able to do so (Michaelian 2010, p. 423).

Shieber is altogether less conciliatory. According to Shieber, this is devastating to internalist approaches. Why? The argument turns on the following inconsistent triad:

(18) The overwhelming majority of listeners are neither sensitive to signs of truth and/or falsity in speakers nor aware of strong reasons for believing what speakers say.

(19) If listeners are neither sensitive to signs of truth and/or falsity in speakers nor aware of strong reasons for believing what speakers say, then they do not come to know things by believing testimony.

(20) The overwhelming majority of listeners do, at least sometimes, come to know things by believing testimony (Shieber 2015, p. 34).

Let us assume that the evidence from social psychology establishes **(18)**.[10] This leaves **(19)** and **(20)**. Broadly speaking, denying **(19)** involves rejecting internalist approaches to testimony, and denying **(20)** involves endorsing a thoroughgoing scepticism about knowledge from testimony. On the face of it, this is a powerful argument against internalist approaches. Scepticism about testimony is highly unintuitive and highly debilitating. Shieber thus points out that 'redressing real world problems often depends on acting on the basis of testimonial evidence, and thus treating such evidence as good enough to justify action. Given this, scepticism regarding testimonial evidence simply isn't a live option' (Shieber 2015, p. 35). Advocates of internalist approaches to testimony are typically disposed to agree with this.[11]

There are, however, at least two ways in which internalists might respond to this argument. The first, as we have already seen, comes from Michaelian and involves pointing out that the fact that beliefs based on testimony are not formed in ways that are sensitive to signs of truth and/or falsity at the time that they are formed does not entail that they are not subsequently sensitive to such signs. This line of response involves detaching the internalist approach from the sceptical outcome. A second line of response, however, is available to the internalist. Where the response from Michaelian seeks to detach the internalist approach from the sceptical outcome, the second response seeks to argue that the claim that the sceptical outcome is problematic is unmotivated.

Suppose that someone managed to show to your satisfaction that your visual faculties in fact do not provide reliable or accurate representations of the world around you. Let us leave aside the question of what the evidence for that would look like, or how someone might manage to do this, and concentrate on the idea that you find yourself presented with convincing evidence that your visual faculties are unreliable. What should you think in such a situation?

You might think one of two things. First, you might think – to your surprise and probable dismay – that your visual faculties in fact do not yield knowledge of the world around you. This might be problematic and distressing for all sorts of reasons, but in the light of evidence showing the unreliability of your visual faculties you might feel compelled to accept it. Alternatively, you might think that – their unreliability notwithstanding – your visual faculties provide you with knowledge of the world around you in some other way. It is not through the reliability of their deliverances, but your visual capacities nonetheless put you in touch with facts about the external world somehow.

What you ought to think in this case is surely straightforward. Faced with compelling evidence that your visual faculties are unreliable, you ought to endorse scepticism about visual perception. The alternative – insisting that your visual capacities must provide you with knowledge in some other way – is just unreasonably dogmatic. Note, however, that the two considerations brought to bear by Shieber in support of the claim that scepticism about testimony is not a live option both apply here. Scepticism about visual perception would be both highly debilitating and also highly unintuitive. These facts notwithstanding, insofar as it is clear that someone ought to endorse scepticism about visual perception in response to the discovery that her visual capacities are unreliable, the fact that scepticism is highly debilitating and also highly unintuitive does not show that it is not a live option.

The idea that the fact that a theory of testimony entails scepticism about testimony counts as a *reductio ad absurdum* against it is thus not straightforward. The above thought experiment shows that, given a sufficiently surprising and debilitating observation, scepticism about testimony can become a plausible hypothesis. It might be that scepticism about testimony is a plausible hypothesis only given a sufficiently surprising and debilitating observation, but given such an observation, scepticism about testimony can become what we ought to endorse. The question, then, becomes whether or not the discovery that listeners are not generally able to monitor speakers for signs of truth and falsity in a reliable way is a sufficiently surprising and debilitating discovery. Without an argument to the conclusion that such a discovery is not sufficiently surprising and debilitating, it is not clear that the discovery that an internalist theory of testimony yields a sceptical outcome constitutes a consideration against it.

Defenders of internalist approaches to testimony might well maintain that the discovery that listeners are unable to distinguish between true and false statements in a reliable way *is* sufficiently surprising and debilitating as to provide a mandate for scepticism about knowledge from testimony. Whilst internalists typically maintain that scepticism about testimony is false, they also maintain that listeners are able to monitor testimony in a reliable way. Moreover, defenders of internalist approaches might well be apt to maintain that these two claims are connected. It is exactly because they are optimistic about the reliability of testimonial monitoring that they are anti-sceptical about the epistemology of testimony. Once it emerges that testimonial monitoring is unreliable, defenders of internalist approaches might insist that the anti-sceptical intuition about testimony also subsides, in much the same way as the anti-sceptical intuition about perception subsides in light of the discovery that one's visual faculties do not yield reliable representations of the world.

The fact that defenders of internalist approaches might insist that the discovery that testimonial monitoring is unreliable is analogous to the discovery that one's visual capacities are unreliable means that the critic of internalism has to come up with a reason for thinking that they are not.

What is wanted is a reason for thinking that the anti-sceptical intuition about testimony survives the discovery that testimonial monitoring is unreliable. Note that, whatever argument the critic comes up with at this juncture will, by itself, be an argument against internalist approaches to testimony. The claim that scepticism about testimony is implausible given the unreliability of testimonial monitoring entails the claim that internalist approaches to testimony are mistaken. So, a reason for the former is a reason for the latter without the evidence from social psychology.

The upshot of this is that the evidence from social psychology does no work in undermining internalist approaches to testimony. Even if the evidence from social psychology establishes the unreliability of testimonial monitoring, and even if this means that internalist approaches to testimony ultimately constitute sceptical approaches to testimony, we cannot get from this observation to the observation that internalist approaches to testimony are problematic without further argument. The fact that testimonial scepticism is implausible prior to the discovery that testimonial monitoring is unreliable does not entail that it is implausible given the unreliability of testimonial monitoring. To argue for this is *eo ipso* to argue against internalist approaches to testimony.

4.4   Circular testimony

I believe, then, that the argument based on the evidence from social psychology fails to undermine internalist approaches to testimony. Where this argument fails, though, another is more successful. The argument that I believe fares better is based on a distinctive type of testimonial situation that I shall call *circular testimony*. Ordinarily, testimonial situations can form chains, where one person tells something to a listener, who tells it to someone else, who tells it to someone else and so on. A testimonial chain becomes circular, however, when someone features in a testimonial chain as a speaker and then subsequently as a listener. A particular type of circular testimony, I argue, presents a problem for internalist approaches to testimony.[12]

Consider a case in which Mia tells her friend Verity that Mikhail Botvinnik beat Tigran Petrosian at the 1963 World Chess Championship. Mia does not believe this and has no reason for believing it. Her testimony is thus mere speculation, but she says it nonetheless. Verity, however, unhesitatingly believes Mia when she tells her this, and, when she subsequently sees her friend Ellie, Verity tells her that Botvinnik beat Petrosian at the 1963 World Chess Championship. Ellie unhesitatingly believes Verity when Verity tells her this, and later, Ellie sees Mia and tells her that Botvinnik beat Petrosian at the 1963 World Chess Championship. Mia has no idea as to why Ellie believes this and no reason to suspect that the testimonial situation is circular, but she is aware of reasons for thinking that Ellie generally says true things. When Ellie tells her, Mia reflects on these reasons and, on the basis of them, comes to believe that Botvinnik beat Petrosian at the 1963 World Chess Championship.

This is an example of circular testimony. It gives rise to the following argument:

(21)   If internalist approaches to testimony are true, then Mia's epistemic grounds for thinking that Botvinnik beat Petrosian at the 1963 World Chess Championship are enhanced when Ellie tells her this.

(22)   Mia's epistemic grounds for thinking that Botvinnik beat Petrosian at the 1963 World Chess Championship are not enhanced when Ellie tells her this.

Therefore

(23)   Internalist approaches to testimony are not true.

The argument is straightforward. **(21)** is a consequence of internalist approaches to testimony. **(22)** is supported by a strong intuition. In the remainder of this section, let us examine the motivations for **(21)** and **(22)**.

The idea behind **(21)** is that, when Ellie tells Mia that Botvinnik beat Petrosian at the 1963 World Chess Championship, Mia has reasons for thinking this that she did not previously have. Her reasons for thinking that Ellie generally says true things become reasons for thinking that Botvinnik beat Petrosian at the 1963 World Chess Championship. Insofar as internalist theories maintain that epistemic grounds are simply reasons that someone is aware of, Ellie telling Mia that Botvinnik beat Petrosian at the 1963 World Chess Championship gives her additional epistemic grounds for this. It is important that Mia is not aware of the circularity in the testimonial situation and nor is this something that she ought to be aware of. If this were not so, then advocates of internalist approaches might maintain that Mia's epistemic grounds are not enhanced because they are defeated. This, however, cannot be the case in the situation described here.

This is why internalist approaches entail that Mia's epistemic grounds are enhanced when she hears Ellie's testimony, as **(21)** states. Of the two premises, however, I suspect that **(21)** is likely to be the less controversial of the two. Internalist responses to the argument are more likely to insist that Mia's epistemic grounds can be enhanced when Ellie tells her that Botvinnik beat Petrosian than to insist that this is not the result of internalist approaches. With this in mind, let us turn our attention to the claim in **(22)**.

One thing that it is important to note in support of **(22)** is that the intermediary links in the testimonial chain – Verity and Ellie – form their beliefs unhesitatingly. In other words, they do not engage in the kind of monitoring that internalist approaches to testimony emphasise the importance of. Rather, they believe what they are told simply because the speaker says so. Verity believes what Mia tells her simply because Mia says it, and Ellie believes what Verity tells her simply because she says it. This is not to say that Verity and Ellie would believe whatever they were told. If Mia had told Verity that she had won the 1963 World Chess Championship, or that the 1963 World Chess Championship took place on the moon, then Verity would not have believed her. But the process that Verity and Ellie go through does not involve reflecting on reasons for thinking that what they are told is true.

In a situation where Verity and Ellie do reflect on their reasons for thinking that what they are told is true, it might be plausible that Mia's epistemic grounds can be enhanced at the end of the case. It is highly plausible that the fact that this seems plausible to both Verity and Ellie means that additional epistemic grounds are made available by Ellie's testimony at the end of the case.[13] This is not, however, plausible in a situation where the intermediary links in the testimonial chain do not reflect independently on what they are told. In such a situation, the speaker essentially receives her own testimony back again via a series of speakers who add nothing to the overall situation.[14]

Knowing that ϕ, or being in a position to know that ϕ, is a matter of being related to the fact that ϕ in a particular way. Someone's epistemic grounds for ϕ are that which put her in a position to know that ϕ. It should be clear in the case under discussion here, though, that Mia is no better related to the fact that Botvinnik beat Petrosian at the 1963 World Chess Championship at the end of the case than she was at the beginning of the case. She is no better related to the fact in question as a result of hearing testimony from someone who herself has no epistemic grounds for it. As such, the internalist view that Mia's epistemic grounds are enhanced in this case is mistaken.

Note that the objection is not that there is no sense in which Mia is better off after hearing Ellie's testimony. In one sense, Mia clearly is better off after hearing Ellie's testimony. Mia is clearly better off in terms of being aware of reasons for thinking that Botvinnik beat Petrosian at the 1963 World Chess Championship. Before Ellie told her this, she was aware of no reasons for believing this, and after Ellie tells her, she is aware of reasons – all her reasons for thinking that Ellie generally says true things become reasons for thinking that Botvinnik beat Petrosian at the 1963 World Chess Championship. The idea that Mia is not better off in any sense is therefore absurd, but the argument here does not depend on this.

Rather, the argument here depends on the claim that Mia is not better off in terms of epistemic grounds. And it is worth noting that the intuition that she is not better off is not unique to transmission theorists. Indeed, as we shall see in §7.3, this intuition gives rise to an argument that has been presented *against* transmission theories. The idea that Mia cannot enhance her epistemic grounds by cycling her belief through the intermediary links in the testimonial chain above is thus one that is amenable to both transmission theorists and their critics. Hence, the argument cannot be resisted by complaining that the intuitions upon which the claim in **(22)** rests are ones that already presuppose the truth of transmission theories.

One might object that, if reasons for believing what a speaker says cannot ground knowledge from testimony in the case above, then it is difficult to see how reasons for believing what the speaker says can *ever* enhance someone's epistemic grounds. But it is clear that, at least sometimes, reasons for believing what a speaker says do enhance someone's epistemic grounds. So, the argument gives rise to a kind of scepticism about reasons for believing testimony that is altogether implausible, but this objection fails.

Intuitively, the reason Mia's epistemic grounds are not enhanced in the above case is that the testimonial situation is circular in a particular way. One might coherently maintain this claim whilst also maintaining that, in a situation where the testimonial situation is not circular and the speaker's testimony is independent of the listener's belief, in the relevant sense, the listener's reasons for believing the speaker can enhance her epistemic grounds and can ground knowledge of what the speaker says.[15] Defenders of internalist approaches to testimony are unable to maintain these two claims. This is because they are committed to thinking – based on the New Evil Demon Argument – that cases that are subjectively indistinguishable are alike with respect to epistemic grounds.

Intuitively, we should think that Mia's epistemic grounds are not enhanced in the case above just because the testimonial situation is circular in a particular way. If the situation were not circular in this way, her epistemic grounds would be enhanced. Yet, the circularity involved in the testimonial situation prevents this. The idea is not merely that Mia fails to know at the end of the case. Rather, the idea is that she is no better connected to the relevant fact. As such, her epistemic grounds are not enhanced. An internalist approach to testimony cannot accommodate this view. Insofar as a case of circular testimony and a case of noncircular testimony can be indistinguishable from the perspective of the listener, internalist approaches insist that they are to be treated in the same way.

4.5 Conclusion

In this chapter, I have been arguing for two main conclusions. The first conclusion is that internalist approaches to the epistemology of testimony are able to withstand the objection based on the evidence from social psychology. Even if the evidence from social psychology shows that listeners are not able to distinguish between true and false statements in a reliable way, it does not show that internalist approaches to the epistemology of testimony are untenable, nor does it provide any additional reason to think that they are untenable over and above what is offered by independent philosophical arguments. The evidence from social psychology undermines internalist approaches to testimony only with the assistance of independent philosophical arguments that, if successful, would undermine internalist approaches to the epistemology of testimony anyway.

The second conclusion that I have been arguing for is that the objection based on circular testimony does undermine internalist approaches to the epistemology of testimony. In virtue of insisting that listeners in subjectively indistinguishable cases are alike with respect to epistemic grounds, internalist approaches are unable to distinguish between cases of circular testimony, in which the listener's epistemic grounds intuitively are not enhanced, and cases of noncircular testimony, in which the listener's epistemic grounds intuitively are enhanced. This is important to the epistemology of testimony, and the internalist inability to distinguish in this way means that internalist approaches to testimony are unable to give a complete account of the epistemology of testimony.

Internalist approaches to testimony are right in one important way. The internalist claim that the reasons that a listener is aware of are important to the epistemology of testimony is surely correct. Furthermore, the importance of reasons that a listener is aware of is not to be explained in terms of these reasons putting a listener in contact with the epistemic grounds that underpin knowledge from testimony. We saw the problems with this view in Chapter 3. Rather, the significance of these reasons is that – as internalist approaches claim – they ground knowledge from testimony. The argument based on circular testimony does not undermine this point, but it does show that internalist approaches to the epistemology of testimony are importantly incomplete.

Notes

1 The original version of the New Evil Demon Argument was presented by Keith Lehrer and Stewart Cohen (1983) and subsequently developed by Cohen (1984). For explicit discussions of these kinds of cases in the epistemology of testimony, see Frederick F. Schmitt (1999), Stephen Wright (2016b) and B.J.C. Madison (2016).

2 The most prominent endorsement of mental-state internalism is given by Earl Conee and Richard Feldman (2004).

3 Epistemological disjunctivist approaches are advocated by John McDowell (1982, 1995, 2002) and Duncan Pritchard (2012). It is applied to the epistemology of testimony by McDowell (1994) and Stephen Wright (forthcoming).

4 Michael Bergmann (2006) argues that mental-state internalism is at odds with the general idea behind internalist approaches to knowledge in general. Discussions of McDowell's (1994) epistemology of testimony from Jennifer Lackey (2008) and Paul Faulkner (2011) identify it as a transmission theory.

5 More recent treatments from Paul Faulkner (1998), Robert Fogelin (2005), Saul Traiger (2010) and Joseph Shieber (2015) argue that this is an inaccurate representation of Hume's views.

6 Responses to this objection come from Jonathan Adler (1994), Jack Lyons (1997) and Tomoji Shogenji (2006).

7 Richard Fumerton (2006) advocates this type of view.

8 Other endorsements come from Peter Lipton (2007) and Anna-Sara Malmgren (2006).

9 Recall the observation from Sanford Goldberg (2010) that silence can be a source of knowledge from Chapter 1.

10 This point is not uncontroversial. Dan Sperber (2013), for example, disputes this.

11 See, for example, Elizabeth Fricker (2006).

12 In doing so, I develop an argument that I originally made in Stephen Wright (2016a).

13 A related point in the epistemology of disagreement is made by Alvin Goldman (2001) and Jennifer Lackey (2013).

14 On the subject of when someone's epistemic position might be enhanced by her own testimony, see Sanford Goldberg (2016).

15 Franz Dietrich and Kai Spiekermann (2013) discuss the sense of independence at issue here.

Bibliography

Adler, J. (1994). Testimony, trust, knowing. *Journal of Philosophy* 91(5), 264–275.

Bergmann, M. (2006). *Justification Without Awareness*. Oxford: Oxford University Press.

Coady, C. A. J. (1992). *Testimony: A Philosophical Study*. Oxford: Clarendon Press.

Coady, C. A. J. (1994). Testimony, observation and "autonomous knowledge". In B. Matilal and A. Chakrabarti (Eds.), *Knowing from Words*, pp. 225–250. Dordrecht: Kluwer Academic Publishers.

Cohen, S. (1984). Justification and truth. *Philosophical Studies* 46(3), 279–295.

Conee, E. and R. Feldman (2004). *Evidentialism*. Oxford: Oxford University Press.

Dietrich, F. and K. Spiekermann (2013). Independent opinions? on the causal foundations of belief formation and jury theorems. *Mind* 122(487), 655–685.

Faulkner, P. (1998). David Hume's reductionist epistemology of testimony. *Pacific Philosophical Quarterly* 39(4), 302–313.

Faulkner, P. (2011). *Knowledge on Trust*. Oxford: Oxford University Press.

Fogelin, R. (2005). *A Defense of Hume on Miracles*. Princeton, NJ: Princeton University Press.

Fricker, E. (1994). Against gullibility. In B. Matilal and A. Chakrabarti (Eds.), *Knowing from Words*, pp. 125–161. Dordrecht: Kluwer Academic Publishers.

Fricker, E. (1995). Critical notice: Telling and trusting: Reductionism and anti-reductionism in the epistemology of testimony. *Mind* 104(414), 393–411.

Fricker, E. (2006). Martians and meetings: Against Burge's neo-Kantian apriorism about testimony. *Philosophica* 78(1), 69–84.

Fumerton, R. (2006). The epistemic role of testimony: Internalist and externalist perspectives. In J. Lackey and E. Sosa (Eds.), *The Epistemology of Testimony*, pp. 77–92. Oxford: Oxford University Press.

Goldberg, S. (2010). *Relying on Others*. Oxford: Oxford University Press.

Goldberg, S. (2016). Can asserting that p improve the speaker's epistemic position (and is that a good thing)? *Australasian Journal of Philosophy* 95(1), 157–170.

Goldman, A. (2001). Experts: Which ones should you trust? *Philosophy and Phenomenological Research* 63(1), 85–110.

Hume, D. (1777). *Enquiries Concerning Human Understanding and the Principles of Morals*. Oxford: Clarendon Press.

Lackey, J. (2008). *Learning from Words: Testimony as a Source of Knowledge*. Oxford: Oxford University Press.

Lackey, J. (2013). Disagreement and belief dependence: Why numbers matter. In D. Christensen and J. Lackey (Eds.), *The Epistemology of Disagreement: New Essays*, pp. 243–266. Oxford: Oxford University Press.

Lehrer, K. and S. Cohen (1983). Justification, truth, and coherence. *Synthese* 55(2), 191–207.

Lipton, P. (2007). Alien abduction: Inference to the best explanation and the management of testimony. *Episteme* 4, 238–251.

Lyons, J. (1997). Testimony, induction and folk psychology. *Australasian Journal of Philosophy* 75(2), 163–178.

Madison, B. (2016). Internalism in the epistemology of testimony redux. *Erkenntnis* 81(4), 741–755.

Malmgren, A. S. (2006). Is there a priori knowledge by testimony? *Philosophical Review* 115(2), 199–241.

McDowell, J. (1982). Criteria, defeasibility, and knowledge. *Proceedings of the British Academy* 68, 435–479.

McDowell, J. (1994). Knowledge by hearsay. In B. Matilal and A. Chakrabarti (Eds.), *Knowing from Words*, pp. 195–224. Dordrecht: Kluwer Academic Publishers.

McDowell, J. (1995). Knowledge and the internal. *Philosophy and Phenomenological Research* 55(4), 877–893.

McDowell, J. (2002). Knowledge and the internal revisited. *Philosophy and Phenomenological Research* 64(1), 97–105.

Michaelian, K. (2010). In defence of gullibility: The epistemology of testimony and the psychology of deception detection. *Synthese* 176(3), 399–427.

Michaelian, K. (2013). The evolution of testimony: Receiver vigilance, speaker honesty and the reliability of communication. *Episteme* 10(1), 37–59.

Pritchard, D. (2012b). *Epistemological Disjunctivism*. Oxford: Oxford University Press.

Schmitt, F. F. (1999). Social epistemology. In J. Greco (Ed.), *The Blackwell Guide to Epistemology*, pp. 354–382. London: Blackwell Publishing.

Shieber, J. (2011). Against credibility. *Australasian Journal of Philosophy* 90(1), 1–18.

Shieber, J. (2015). *Testimony: A Philosophical Introduction*. London: Routledge.

Shogenji, T. (2006). A defense of reductionism about testimonial justification of beliefs. *Noûs* 40(2), 331–346.

Sperber, D. (2013). Speakers are honest because hearers are vigilant. *Episteme* 10(1), 61–71.

Traiger, S. (2010). Experience and testimony in Hume's philosophy. *Episteme* 7(1), 42–57.

Wright, S. (2016a). Circular testimony. *Philosophical Studies* 173(8), 2029–2048.

Wright, S. (2016b). Internalism in the epistemology of testimony. *Erkenntnis* 81(1), 69–86.

Wright, S. (forthcoming). Testimonial disjunctivism. In C. Doyle, J. Milburn and D. Pritchard (Eds.), *Epistemological Disjunctivism*. London: Routledge.

5   Reliabilist approaches

5.1   Introduction

Instead of taking an internalist approach to the epistemology of testimony, one might take a reliabilist approach. Their substantial differences notwithstanding, there are a number of fundamental similarities between internalist and reliabilist approaches to testimony. Both take it that knowledge from testimony is fundamentally similar to knowledge from instruments, both maintain that it is possible to give an adequate account of testimony without appeal to transmission and both are the product of applying approaches to epistemology in general to the domain of testimony.

Reliabilist approaches to epistemology in general endorse the following claim:

(R)   A subject's epistemic grounds for ϕ are a matter of the reliability of the processes involved in the production of her belief that ϕ.

Applying this to the epistemology of testimony yields the following:

(TR)   A listener's epistemic grounds for ϕ are a matter of the reliability of the processes associated with believing the speaker's testimony that ϕ.

Unlike defenders of internalist approaches, defenders of reliabilist approaches reject the claim that the fact that two testimonial situations are subjectively indistinguishable means that the listeners are alike with respect to epistemic grounds in each case. Reliabilist approaches are thus apt to return the intuitively correct account of the circular testimony cases that undermine internalist approaches. Nonetheless, in the same way that the statement of internalist approaches to testimony given in §4.1 raised questions concerning what it means for a reason to be internal to a listener and what reasons are plausibly internal to a listener, the statement in (TR) raises questions of what a process being reliable amounts to and which processes are relevant to a listener's epistemic grounds.

The former question is complicated but – as far as I can tell – ultimately unproblematic. In §2.2 we saw the difference between approaches to epistemology that emphasise reliability and those that emphasise safety or sensitivity. The central idea, in each case, is that what matters is the modal profile of the processes involved in the production of the subject's belief. For the purposes of this discussion, we can leave aside the question of whether we should think in terms of reliability, safety or sensitivity. The latter question, however, leads to problems for reliabilist approaches to testimony. Reliabilist approaches to testimony fail because they must give an account of which processes are relevant to a listener's epistemic grounds in any particular case. And the most plausible answer ultimately undermines the view that epistemic grounds are a matter of reliable processes. The problem here superficially resembles the generality problem, but I shall argue that the objection here is not merely the generality problem by another name. Rather, it is an independent objection to reliabilist approaches to the epistemology of testimony.

5.2 Reliabilism and the epistemology of testimony

Like internalist approaches to testimony, reliabilist approaches have no use for the idea that testimony transmits knowledge and epistemic grounds. The reliabilist strategy for dispensing with transmission, however, differs from the internalist strategy. Internalist approaches are apt to maintain that transmission in the epistemology of testimony is outright false. According to internalist approaches, epistemic grounds are a matter of what someone is aware of, and since a listener is not made aware of a speaker's reasons by her testimony, testimony does not transmit knowledge and epistemic grounds.[1] By contrast, reliabilist approaches – whether they are construed in terms of reliability, sensitivity or safety – maintain not that claims of transmission are false, but that they add nothing to that which is already accounted for perfectly well by reliabilist approaches (and insofar as they do, they go wrong).

Reliabilists are typically disposed towards thinking that the fact that a speaker knows or has epistemic grounds for what she says can be a significant epistemic feature of a testimonial situation. Furthermore, it can be that the listener comes to know what the speaker says or has epistemic grounds for it because the speaker knows or has epistemic grounds for it. A speaker might know that ϕ, intend to inform a listener with respect to ϕ and thereby come to bring the listener to know that ϕ. Her testimony being epistemically sincere might lead to it being reliable and thus making knowledge and epistemic grounds available to a listener. However, reliabilist approaches maintain that the way to explain this is in terms of reliability, not in terms of transmission.

At this point, one might think that there is little difference between reliabilist and transmission approaches to testimony. This appearance becomes more vivid when we recall that, in Chapter 2, I argued a speaker's testimony makes knowledge and epistemic grounds available to transmit only if the speaker's testimony is epistemically sincere – i.e., when the reason why she says something is the fact that she has epistemic grounds for it. However, we have already seen that the fact that a speaker's testimony is epistemically sincere does not entail that it is reliably produced. We saw this in cases where a speaker produces epistemically sincere testimony under the watch of someone who would have intervened had she tried to say something different, so that her testimony does not have the modal profile associated with reliable testimony. In such cases, transmission theorists should allow that the speaker's testimony makes knowledge and epistemic grounds available to the listener, where reliabilist approaches should reject it.

These cases show that transmission theories and reliabilist theories are not extensionally the same. They are not merely two different ways of describing the same phenomena. In Chapter 8, we shall consider cases in which a speaker's testimony might be reliable without making knowledge and epistemic grounds available to transmit. For the purpose of the discussion in this chapter, however, it is important to keep in view the kind of cases in which transmission theorists should maintain that knowledge and epistemic grounds are made available by a speaker's testimony, but advocates of reliabilist approaches are apt to deny this. It is these that will provide the foundation of the argument against reliabilist approaches.

With this in mind, let us turn to the question of which processes are relevant to a listener's epistemic grounds. In a testimonial situation where a listener forms a belief in response to a speaker's testimony, there are two sets of cognitive processes. There are those situated in the speaker. These terminate with an output in the form of the speaker's testimony. There are also those situated in the listener. These begin with the listener hearing the speaker's testimony and terminate with an output in the form of a belief. The reliability of each set of processes is independent of the other. One might think that, *pace* the evidence from social psychology discussed in §4.3, a listener might be able to distinguish between true and false statements even though the speaker's testimony is merely speculation and thus unreliably produced. Alternatively, one might think that a speaker could produce reliable testimony even though the listener is unable to distinguish between true and false statements, making the listener's comprehension processes unreliable, regardless of the reliability of the processes involved in the production of the speaker's testimony.

This gives rise to the question of which processes are relevant to a listener's epistemic grounds. What should we think in a case where the speaker's testimony is reliably produced, but the listener's comprehension processes are unreliable, or vice versa? Also, what should we think in a case where both the processes involved in the production of the speaker's testimony and the listener's comprehension processes are reliable – which ones are relevant to the listener's epistemic grounds? Let us call this the question of testimonial reliability. I shall argue that considering this question brings out a problem for reliabilist approaches to testimony.

Four obvious answers present themselves:

(TR$_1$) Knowledge from testimony is grounded in and depends on the reliability of the processes involved in the production of the speaker's testimony.

(TR$_2$) Knowledge from testimony is grounded in and depends on the reliability of the processes involved in the listener's comprehension of the speaker's testimony.

(TR$_3$) Knowledge from testimony is grounded in and depends on both the reliability of the processes involved in the production of the speaker's testimony and the reliability of the processes involved in the listener's comprehension of the speaker's testimony.

(TR$_4$) Knowledge from testimony is grounded in and depends on either the reliability of the processes involved in the production of the speaker's testimony or the reliability of the processes involved in the listener's comprehension of the speaker's testimony.

I believe that none of these answers is satisfactory. The argument that I shall develop has the following form:

(24) The most plausible answer to the question of testimonial reliability is **(TR$_4$)**.

(25) If **(TR$_4$)** is true, then the epistemology of testimony cannot adequately be characterised without appeal to transmission.

(26) If the epistemology of testimony cannot adequately be characterised without appeal to transmission, then reliabilist approaches to the epistemology of testimony are false.

Therefore

(27) Reliabilist approaches to the epistemology of testimony are false.

I shall come to the case for **(24)** in the next section and the case for **(25)** in §5.4. At this juncture, however, a comment on **(26)** is in order.

It is important to distinguish between **(26)**, as it appears in the above argument, and the following claim:

(26*) If the epistemology of testimony cannot adequately be characterised purely in terms of reliable processes, then reliabilist approaches to the epistemology of testimony are false.[2]

The difference between **(26)** and **(26*)** is subtle, but important. It is brought out in a recent exchange between Elizabeth Fricker (2015) and Jennifer Lackey (2015). In arguing against reliabilist approaches to the epistemology of testimony, Fricker claims that reliabilist approaches to testimony are committed to the idea that all that matters in the epistemology of testimony is process reliability. Other facts matter only insofar as they contribute to reliability (Fricker 2015, p. 187). In response, Lackey points out that not all reliabilist approaches are so unsophisticated. Reliabilist approaches, Lackey notes, emphasise the importance of various features, such as the intellectual virtues manifested by the speaker and listener and the environment in which the testimonial exchange takes place (Lackey 2015, p. 204).

As we shall see subsequently, Lackey's response to Fricker's case against reliabilist approaches to the epistemology of testimony ultimately falters. Yet, the observation that reliabilist theories are not simply interested in considerations concerning reliability is fundamentally correct. The argument that I have outlined, however, does not rest on the premise that reliabilist approaches are exclusively interested in considerations about reliability. Rather, it rests on the premise that reliabilist approaches do not incorporate a notion of transmission into their views. This much is correct. Where reliabilist approaches are not so unsubtle as to simply focus exclusively on reliability, they do not take a notion of transmission to feature in an adequate epistemology of testimony. The argument that I advance here is therefore not directed simply against implausibly unsophisticated reliabilist approaches, in the way that Lackey maintains that Fricker's argument is.

It is also worth noting at this stage that the argument I have outlined has similarities with the objection to reliabilist approaches known as the generality problem. The two, however, are not to be conflated.[3] The generality problem, I believe, is plausibly a problem for any epistemological theory (and plausibly also a problem for other theories beyond the realm of epistemology, too).[4] As far as the discussion here is concerned, the generality problem might undermine reliabilist approaches to the epistemology of testimony. But it is difficult, I suggest, to see how it is a problem for reliabilist approaches to testimony specifically, rather than to reliabilist approaches to epistemology in general. The objection that I present here is one that does not apply to reliabilist approaches to epistemology in general.[5]

The generality problem is typically taken to have its roots in discussions during the 1980s.[6] In a 1929 discussion, however, F.P. Ramsey, despite expressing a sympathy for a reliabilist approach to epistemology, expresses a dissatisfaction with the idea of a process that might be taken to carry the seeds of the generality problem.[7] The generality problem begins with the observation that any individual instance of belief formation will be an instance of various process types. Recall the observation from C.A.J. Coady (1992) in §4.2 that a report of a sick lion in Taronga Park Zoo could be identified in various different ways. A related observation gets the generality problem started. As far as the generality problem is concerned, the problem is not just that a listener might *identify* testimony as an instance of various different types, but the fact that the speaker's testimony *is* an instance of these various types. The problem is not just that a listener might have different *reasons* concerning the reliability of each type, but that the reliability of each type will *in fact* be different.

Those who advance the generality problem argue that this undermines reliabilist approaches. If there is no fact about what process a particular instance of belief formation is an instance of, then there is no fact about the reliability of the process that a particular instance of belief formation is an instance of, and if there is no fact about the reliability of the relevant process, then an approach to epistemology that is fundamentally about process reliability is going to be problematic. Like the generality problem, the objection here concerns the identity of the relevant processes in a testimonial situation. The difference between the argument here and the one associated with the generality problem, however, can be brought out by two closely related observations.

First, and most simply, the objection here does not concern levels of generality. The objection here concerns identifying which set of processes are relevant to a listener's epistemic grounds. With the generality problem, the idea is that we have the relevant processes in view but are unclear about the appropriate level of generality at which to characterise them. The objection here is that it is not clear which set of processes are the relevant ones to have in view in a testimonial exchange. Second – and relatedly – even if we stipulate a solution to the generality problem and insist on describing processes at a certain level of generality, the problem here still persists.[8] Even if we agree on the relevant level of generality at which to evaluate processes for reliability, we are still left with the question of whether we should be evaluating the processes involved in the production of the speaker's testimony or the listener's comprehension processes.

This is why the objection here is distinct from the generality problem, though the two are closely related. With this in mind, we can move to the motivation for **(24)**.

5.3   Production processes and comprehension processes

In principle, there are four answers to the question of testimonial reliability available to advocates of reliabilist approaches. These are detailed in **(TR₁)**, **(TR₂)**, **(TR₃)** and **(TR₄)**. Of these, however, the first two seem to be at odds with the central idea behind reliabilist approaches. In virtue of this, both can be undermined by similar arguments. The view in **(TR₁)** is a popular one.[9] Against it, though, we might consider a case in which a speaker's testimony is mere speculation. It happens to be true, but it is unreliably produced. The listener, however, is able to distinguish between true and false statements in a reliable way. The listener thus recognises the speaker's testimony as true and forms a belief in what she says.

As we saw in §4.3, the evidence from social psychology indicates that human beings are not typically able to distinguish between true and false statements in this way, but we have already encountered this type of case in §3.3, and this gives us an idea of what reliabilist approaches ought to maintain in this case. It seems clear that reliabilist approaches ought to maintain that the relevant processes are those involved in the listener's comprehension of the speaker's testimony. The unreliability of the speaker's testimony notwithstanding, it seems possible that the listener can come to know what the speaker says in virtue of her capacity to distinguish between true and false statements in a reliable way.

What should those who advocate **(TR₁)** make of this case? One answer is given by Lackey. We have already seen that, in such a case, Lackey maintains that the speaker's testimony is not the source of the listener's knowledge but rather a trigger of it (Lackey 2008, p. 92). In this spirit, a reliabilist who endorses **(TR₁)** might maintain that knowledge from testimony is grounded in the reliability of the processes involved in the production of the speaker's testimony, but that this type of case is not an instance of knowledge *from* testimony, so much as an instance of knowledge *triggered by* testimony.

Nevertheless, this response is inadequate. Insofar as we want to distinguish between knowledge based on testimony and knowledge triggered by testimony, the business of the epistemology of testimony is accounting for both. The starting observation for philosophical interest in the epistemology of testimony is that, a lot of the time, believing what someone says results in knowledge. But this starting observation is neutral between the idea that knowledge from testimony is a matter of testimony being a source of knowledge and testimony being a trigger of knowledge. Indeed, the question of whether testimony primarily acts as a source of knowledge or as a trigger of knowledge might be one way of thinking about what is at issue between internalist approaches to testimony and transmission theorists. We thus cannot maintain **(TR$_1$)** on the grounds that, where the relevant processes seem to be those involved in the listener's comprehension of the speaker's testimony, the case is one of testimony triggering knowledge rather than being a source of knowledge.

Another alternative comes from Peter Graham's discussions of reliability and testimony. Against the evidence from social psychology, Graham maintains that a listener's comprehension processes can be reliable in such a way that she is able to distinguish between true and false statements. Rather than grounding knowledge from testimony, however, Graham suggests that the reliability of a listener's comprehension processes should be thought of in terms of providing a *prima facie* and *pro tanto* entitlement to believe what a speaker says (Graham 2010, pp. 149–150). Furthermore, Graham notes elsewhere that a *prima facie* and *pro tanto* epistemic support need not amount to a full epistemic ground – the kind that can ground knowledge from testimony – even in the absence of countervailing considerations (Graham 2006b, p. 108). The epistemic grounds that underpin the listener's knowledge, according to Graham, come from the reliability of the processes involved in the production of the speaker's testimony.[10]

This, however, seems out of line with reliabilist approaches. Insofar as reliabilist approaches insist that the epistemic grounds that support knowledge from testimony are a matter of reliable processes, it seems that they ought not to restrict the scope of the reliability of comprehension processes to providing a merely *prima facie* and *pro tanto* epistemic ground. Rather, it seems as though the listener's comprehension processes, insofar as they are sufficiently reliable, should be able to provide epistemic grounds sufficient to put someone in a position to know the truth of what the speaker says. One might find it intuitive that a listener's comprehension processes, no matter how reliable, cannot put someone in the right kind of relationship to the fact the speaker reports to ground knowledge from testimony (I do not find this intuitive). Yet, to the extent that this is intuitive, it indicates that the general idea behind reliabilist approaches to testimony is mistaken.

It is cases in which a listener's comprehension processes are reliable, but the processes involved in the production of the speaker's testimony are not, that cast doubt on **(TR$_1$)**. The opposite case seems to make difficulties for advocates of **(TR$_2$)**. Suppose that a speaker produces testimony that is highly reliable, but the listener simply believes whatever she is told. In such a case, it seems that the relevant processes are those involved in the production of the speaker's testimony, *contra* **(TR$_2$)**. Whilst **(TR$_2$)** has fewer advocates that $(\mathbf{TR_1})$, there is a line of response open to the defender of $(\mathbf{TR_2})$ that is not open to the defender of $(\mathbf{TR_1})$. I do not believe that it is successful, but it is worth considering.

Ramsey, in his brief discussion of reliabilism, points out that the reliability of inferential processes depends on their inputs. Alvin Goldman (1979), in a landmark paper outlining reliabilism, distinguishes between *conditional* and *unconditional* reliability. A process is conditionally reliable insofar as it reliably yields true outputs, given a certain quality of input. A process is unconditionally reliable insofar as it reliably yields true outputs regardless of the quality of its inputs. Deductive reasoning, for example, is conditionally reliable since it reliably yields true outputs given true inputs. It is not, however, unconditionally reliable since it does not reliably yield true outputs in cases where its inputs are false.

In defence of $(\mathbf{TR_2})$, one might point out that, in the kind of case under discussion, the listener's comprehension processes are conditionally reliable. Insofar as the listener merely believes whatever she is told, her comprehension processes reliably yield true beliefs in cases where the speaker's testimony is reliably produced. In cases where the speaker's testimony is not reliably produced, the listener's comprehension processes do not reliably yield true outputs. Regarding the kind of case under discussion here, a defender of $(\mathbf{TR_2})$ might suggest that the listener's comprehension processes are (conditionally) reliable, and it is *this* reliability that grounds the listener's knowledge in this case.

This accommodates the idea that the reliability of the processes involved in the listener's comprehension of the speaker's testimony is important, but it does so in a highly unsatisfying way. Explaining the case in terms of the conditional reliability of the listener's comprehension processes involves accepting that the real source of the reliability that grounds the listener's knowledge is the reliability of the processes involved in the production of the speaker's testimony. The result is that both $(\mathbf{TR_1})$ and $(\mathbf{TR_2})$ ultimately collapse into versions of $(\mathbf{TR_4})$. Advocates of $(\mathbf{TR_1})$ need to appeal to the reliability of the listener's comprehension processes in cases where these are reliable, despite the unreliability of the processes involved in the production of the speaker's testimony. Advocates of $(\mathbf{TR_2})$, on the other hand, need to appeal to the reliability of the processes involved in the production of the speaker's testimony to account for cases in which a speaker's testimony is reliably produced, and the listener's comprehension processes are conditionally reliable.

What about $(\mathbf{TR_3})$? On the face of it, the above arguments against $(\mathbf{TR_1})$ and $(\mathbf{TR_2})$ are arguments against $(\mathbf{TR_3})$. The arguments against $(\mathbf{TR_1})$ and $(\mathbf{TR_2})$ purport to show that the reliability of *either* set of processes can ground knowledge. Since $(\mathbf{TR_3})$ maintains that the reliability of *both* sets of processes is necessary for knowledge from testimony, it is vulnerable to the same objections placed against (TR_1) and (TR_2). Now, I believe that this line of reasoning is sound, but Sanford Goldberg (2010) has endorsed (TR_3) on the grounds that the above arguments fail. In the remainder of this section, let us consider Goldberg's case.

On the subject of the case in which the speaker's testimony is unreliably produced but the listener's comprehension processes are unconditionally reliable, Goldberg considers a case in which the speaker sees something in a way not quite sufficient to put her in a position to know it. About this case, Goldberg says the following:

> It should be patent that the hearer's testimonial belief fails to amount to knowledge [. . .] The hearer's true testimonial belief is no better related to the truth than was the testimony on which it was based. Since the testimony itself was not quite good enough [. . .] it would seem patent that the hearer's belief, which was based on that not-quite-good-enough testimony, does not amount to knowledge. The cost of denying this would be considerable. After all, it would be a curious process indeed that turned what in the mind/brain of the source was a belief that was not quite reliable enough to count as knowledge into what in the mind/brain of the hearer is a belief whose reliability suffices for knowledge – and this, despite the fact that from an epistemic point of view the hearer was less well placed regarding the truth of the proposition than was her source!
>
> (Goldberg 2010, pp. 98–99)

There are three points that might be made in response to this. First, it might be significant that Goldberg describes the belief as *based on* the speaker's testimony. The thought might be that, in the kind of case where the listener's knowledge is intuitively grounded in the reliability of her comprehension processes, the listener's knowledge depends on the reliability of both sets of processes. This is an analogue of the view inspired by Lackey that we have already discussed in considering (TR_1), and the same point can be made here in response. The datum to be explained is knowledge gained by believing what speakers say. This encompasses both cases in which the listener's knowledge is based on the speaker's testimony in a strong sense and cases in which it is not.

Second, Goldberg notes that the listener is, from an epistemic point of view, less well-placed than the speaker. The idea is that the speaker saw what she says, albeit in non-ideal circumstances, whereas the listener simply has the speaker's word for it that what she says is the case. But the fact that the listener only has the speaker's word for it when the speaker saw it does not entail that the listener is in a worse epistemic position than the speaker. Indeed, one might think that the reverse is true. The listener is in possession of something that she recognises as a reliable indication of what the speaker says – the speaker's testimony. The speaker, by contrast, is in a position where her perceptual experience is not ideal. There is thus reason to doubt the claim that the listener is less well-placed regarding the fact that the speaker reports.

Third, Goldberg notes that the processes involved in the listener's comprehension must be 'curious' ones. This is particularly true given the evidence from social psychology, but the fact that these processes are curious does not show that they are impossible. The apparent coherence of the kind of case being discussed gives us reason to think that such comprehension processes, curious or otherwise, are at least possible, and the evidence from social psychology only provides evidence that the claim that listeners generally have such processes is contingently false. It is thus far from obvious that the kind of case in question here is beyond the scope of an epistemological theory of testimony.

Goldberg also objects to the idea that the reliability of the processes involved in the production of the speaker's testimony can, by itself, ground knowledge from testimony. In doing so, Goldberg draws an analogy with memory, comparing two memory processes, M_1 and M_2. Both processes transform apparent memories into beliefs. But where M_1 produces beliefs whether or not the inputs are true, M_2 includes a mechanism that limits the false outputs it produces. When its inputs are false, M_2 only produces outputs 5% of the time. Intuitively, M_2 is the more reliable process, and importantly, this is so even when the inputs are reliably produced. M_2's capacity for limiting the false outputs it yields means that its outputs have an additional reliability that the outputs from M_1 do not have. What is more, Goldberg points out that in the case of a third memory process, M_3, which has no filter but is provided with unreliable inputs 99% of the time, even the 1% of true outputs that it yields are unreliably produced (Goldberg 2010, pp. 120–124).

The general idea is that, even in cases where one set of processes is highly reliable, it is intuitive that the other set being unconditionally reliable contributes to the overall reliability of the eventual outputs. This point is well made. It is important, however, to be careful about exactly what this establishes. It shows that the overall reliability of the processes that give rise to beliefs will often be a function of both the processes involved in the production of the speaker's testimony and the processes involved in the listener's comprehension. It shows that outputs from cases where both sets of processes are reliable will often be more reliable than those from cases where only one set of processes is reliable. But it does not, one might think, show that knowledge – understood as being in a particular kind of relation to a fact – depends on the unconditional reliability of both sets of processes.

By way of illustration, we might consider a fourth memory process, M_4. Like M_3, M_4 yields outputs whether its inputs are true or false. Unlike M_3, however, M_4 operates in an environment where it is provided with reliable inputs 99% of the time. This raises the question of what we should say about M_4. We might say that it is a flawed memory process. We should certainly say that its outputs could be more reliable, but on the assumption that the kind of reliability required for knowledge is anything short of 100% reliability, we should think that the outputs from M_4 can amount to knowledge. Therefore, the fact that beliefs that are the outputs in cases where both sets of processes being unconditionally reliable are more reliably produced than beliefs formed in cases where only one set of processes is reliable does not entail that the reliability of both the processes involved in the production of the speaker's testimony and the processes involved in the listener's comprehension of the speaker's testimony is required for knowledge from testimony, as **(TR₃)** states.

Ultimately, the claims in **(TR₁)**, **(TR₂)** and **(TR₃)** are each problematic. The claim in **(TR₁)** is problematic because there are cases in which processes relevant to the listener's knowledge are intuitively those involved in the listener's comprehension, rather than those involved in the production of the speaker's testimony. Equally, the claim in **(TR₂)** is problematic because there are cases in which the processes relevant to the listener's knowledge are intuitively those involved in the production of the speaker's testimony, rather than those involved in the listener's comprehension.

The claim in **(TR₃)** is problematic because, in the same way that it is intuitive that there are cases in which the relevant processes to a listener's knowledge are those situated in the speaker and cases in which the relevant processes to a listener's knowledge are those situated in the listener, there are cases in which the reliability of either set of processes is intuitively sufficient for knowledge according to reliabilist standards. This leaves **(TR₄)** – the approach that claims that knowledge from testimony depends on either the reliability of the processes involved in the production of the speaker's testimony or the reliability of the processes involved in the listener's comprehension of the speaker's testimony. On the face of it, **(TR₄)** is not undermined by the cases in which one set of processes seems to be sufficient for knowledge. This gives us the case for **(24)**.

5.4   The disjunctive approach

I believe that advocates of reliabilist approaches to the epistemology of testimony should endorse **(TR₄)**, but I also believe that **(TR₄)** is problematic.

Endorsing **(TR$_4$)** gives rise to another question, which concerns when the relevant processes are those involved in the production of the speaker's testimony and when they are the processes involved in the listener's comprehension of the speaker's testimony. As we have seen, the reliability of each set of processes is independent of the other. So the question of which set of processes is relevant in which case is important.

The correct answer, I believe, is supplied by Ernest Sosa's (2010) discussion of testimony as a source of knowledge.[11] Sosa advocates **(TR$_1$)** – the view that the relevant processes are those involved in the production of the speaker's testimony. In doing so, Sosa compares the epistemology of testimony with the epistemology of instruments. In cases where we know things on the basis of instruments, our knowledge is grounded in the reliability of the processes involved in the production of the instrument's deliverance. Why? According to Sosa, we implicitly assume that the instrument is reliable in forming our beliefs on the basis of its deliverances. In Sosa's words, 'in thus relying, we make manifest the assumption of reliability' (Sosa 2010, p. 131). We may have no assumption of how or why a particular instrument is reliable, but we assume nonetheless that it is reliable. In the same way with a speaker, we may not have any view as to why her testimony is reliably produced, but even so, we maintain that it is reliably produced.

To make an assumption in this way is not to use the belief that the speaker's testimony is reliably produced as a premise in one's reasoning.[12] Rather, in terms of the vocabulary introduced in Chapter 1, it is to attempt to believe what the speaker says in such a way that the reason why one believes it is the fact that the speaker's testimony is reliably produced. Of course, in a situation where the speaker's testimony is not reliably produced, a listener cannot succeed in this enterprise, for there is no fact to be the reason why she believes what the speaker says. In such situations, the reason why the listener believes what the speaker says is the fact that she *believes* that the speaker's testimony is reliably produced. Note that this is not the same as *inferring* the truth of what the speaker says through the premise that her testimony is reliably produced, in which case the reason why the listener believes what the speaker says is the fact that she has reasons for thinking that the speaker's testimony is reliably produced.

It is easy to see how this idea can be extended. In a case where the listener forms her belief through the assumption that the speaker's testimony is reliably produced, it is the reliability of the processes involved in the production of the speaker's testimony that is relevant – and *this* reliability that grounds the listener's knowledge in a case where the listener comes to be in a position to know as a result. In a situation where the listener forms her belief through the assumption that her comprehension processes are reliable, it is the reliability of *these* processes that is relevant, and in a situation where the listener comes to know in this way her knowledge is grounded in the reliability of *these* processes. I believe that this idea is fundamentally correct and is what the advocate of (TR_4) should maintain. It is, however, problematic.

Not all assumptions reduce to assumptions about reliability. A listener might believe what a speaker says on the assumption that the speaker *knows* what she says or *has epistemic grounds* for what she says. As we have seen, the speaker knowing or having epistemic grounds for what she says is logically independent of the speaker producing reliable testimony, even if the speaker's testimony is epistemically sincere. The result is that an assumption of knowledge or epistemic grounds – which we might call an *epistemic* assumption – cannot be reduced to an assumption of reliability. Insofar as the idea that what grounds a listener's knowledge is determined by the assumptions she makes in believing what the speaker says, we need an account of what grounds knowledge gained through an epistemic assumption.

Whatever it is, it cannot be the reliability of a process, since an epistemic assumption does not reduce to an assumption of reliability. The natural answer, I suggest, is that it is grounded in the speaker's epistemic grounds for what she says. In believing through an epistemic assumption, the reason why the listener believes what the speaker says is the fact that the speaker knows or has epistemic grounds for what she says. This is a way of saying that the speaker's knowledge and/or epistemic grounds are transmitted to the listener. One way of resisting this idea might be to suggest that, in a case where the listener forms her belief through an epistemic assumption, she does not come to know. However, it is hard to see how a reliabilist could make this argument without begging the question. The natural answer – because knowledge is grounded in reasons that one is aware of and thus beliefs formed through assumptions do not amount to knowledge at all – is an internalist idea that is not available to reliabilists. Another answer – because only reliability can ground knowledge – simply begs the question.

This gives us the motivation for **(25)**. The most plausible account of which processes are relevant is one that treats the identity of the relevant set of processes as a function of the assumption that the listener makes in forming her belief. Not all assumptions are assumptions of reliability, though. Some assumptions are epistemic assumptions. Hence, not all knowledge from testimony is grounded in the reliability of processes. Some assumptions are distinctively epistemic assumptions. This means that knowledge from testimony is, at least sometimes, grounded in the speaker's knowledge and epistemic grounds.

5.5   Conclusion

I have been arguing that reliabilist approaches are unable to give an adequate account of the epistemic grounds that underpin knowledge from testimony. As with internalist approaches, the problem is not that reliabilist approaches are unable to account for *any* knowledge from testimony. I believe that they are able to do this. I also believe that the cases that they account for cannot be explained in any other non-reliabilist terms.

The trouble, however, is that reliabilist approaches are unable to account for *all* knowledge from testimony. Whilst there are cases in which knowledge from testimony is grounded in reliability, making sense of this appears to leave open the possibility that there are also cases in which knowledge from testimony is grounded in factors other than those associated with the reliability of processes. Specifically, there are cases in which knowledge from testimony is grounded in the transmission of knowledge and epistemic grounds.

Notes

1 An interesting point of comparison here concerns David James Barnett's (2015) recent argument to the conclusion that this marks a substantial difference between testimony and memory as epistemic sources. According to Barnett, memory *does* make reasons available in a way that testimony does not. The result is that the case for preservationism about memory is stronger than the case for transmission about testimony. Cf. Tyler Burge (1993, 1997), Michael Dummett (1994) and David Owens (2000).

2 Of course, employing **(26*)** in the argument would also involve the following modified version of **(25)**:

> **(25*)** If **(TR₄)** is true, then the epistemology of testimony cannot adequately be characterised purely in terms of reliable processes.

3 Sanford Goldberg (2010) anticipates the argument that I make here and suggests that it is similar to the generality problem.

4 On the subject of whether the generality problem presents a particular problem for reliabilist approaches, see Michael Bishop (2010), Earl Conee (2013) and Juan Comesaña (2006).

5 It might extend beyond the epistemology of testimony to the epistemology of memory, for example, but it does not extend to sources of knowledge in which there is only one set of cognitive processes.

6 Specifically, discussions from Richard Feldman (1985) and Richard Foley (1985).

7 See Ramsey (1990).

8 Attempts at solving the generality problem are given by William Alston (1995), James R. Beebe (2004) and Mark Heller (1995).

9 Advocates of (TR₁) include Fred Dretske (1982), Peter Graham (2000a, 2000b, 2006a), Jennifer Lackey (2008) and Ernest Sosa (2010).

10 See Peter Graham (2000a, 2000b, 2006a) on the subject of the reliability of the processes involved in the production of the speaker's testimony.

11 I discuss Sosa's epistemology of testimony elsewhere in Stephen Wright (2014).
12 As we saw in Chapter 3, if the listener *does* use the belief as a premise in her reasoning, then it is difficult to see how the epistemic grounds that support the speaker's testimony extend beyond these reasons to include the reliability of the processes in question.

Bibliography

Alston, W. (1995). How to think about reliability. *Philosophical Topics* 23(1), 1–29.

Barnett, D. J. (2015). Is memory merely the testimony from one's former self? *Philosophical Review* 124(3), 353–392.

Beebe, J. R. (2004). The generality problem, statistical relevance and the tri-level hypothesis. *Noûs* 38(1), 177–195.

Bishop, M. (2010). Why the generality problem is everybody's problem. *Philosophical Studies* 151(2), 285–298.

Burge, T. (1993). Content preservation. *Philosophical Review* 102(4), 457–488.

Burge, T. (1997). Interlocution, perception, and memory. *Philosophical Studies* 86(1), 21–47.

Coady, C. A. J. (1992). *Testimony: A Philosophical Study*. Oxford: Clarendon Press.

Comesaña, J. (2006). A well-founded solution to the generality problem. *Philosophical Studies* 129(1), 27–47.

Conee, E. (2013). The specificity of the generality problem. *Philosophical Studies* 151(2), 751–762.

Dretske, F. (1982). A cognitive cul-de-sac. *Mind* 91(361), 109–111.

Dummett, M. (1994). Testimony and memory. In B. Matilal and A. Chakrabarti (Eds.), *Knowing from Words*, pp. 251–272. Dordrecht: Kluwer Academic Publishers.

Feldman, R. (1985). Reliability and justification. *The Monist* 68(2), 159–174.

Foley, R. (1985). What's Wrong with Reliabilism? *The Monist* 68(2), 188–202.

Fricker, E. (2015). How to make invidious distinctions amongst reliable testifiers. *Episteme* 12(2), 173–202.

Goldberg, S. (2010). *Relying on Others*. Oxford: Oxford University Press.

Goldman, A. (1979). What is justified belief? In G. Pappas (Ed.), *Knowledge and Justification*, pp. 1–23. Dordrecht: D. Reidel Publishing Company.

Graham, P. (2000a). Conveying information. *Synthese* 30(3), 365–392.

Graham, P. (2000b). Transferring knowledge. *Noûs* 34(1), 131–152.

Graham, P. (2006a). Can testimony generate knowledge? *Philosophica* 78(2), 105–127.

Graham, P. (2006b). Liberal fundamentalism and its rivals. In J. Lackey and E. Sosa (Eds.), *The Epistemology of Testimony*, pp. 92–115. Oxford: Oxford University Press.

Graham, P. (2010). Testimonial entitlement and the function of comprehension. In A. Haddock, A. Millar and D. Pritchard (Eds.), *Social Epistemology*, pp. 148–174. Oxford: Oxford University Press.

Heller, M. (1995). The simple solution to the generality problem. *Noûs* 29(4), 501–515.

Lackey, J. (2008). *Learning from Words*. Oxford: Oxford University Press.

Lackey, J. (2015). Reliability and knowledge in the epistemology of testimony. *Episteme* 12(2), 203–208.

Owens, D. (2000). *Reason Without Freedom: The Problem of Epistemic Normativity*. London: Routledge.

Ramsey, F. P. (1990). Knowledge. In F. P. Ramsey and D. H. Mellor (Eds.), *Philosophical Papers*, pp. 110–111. Cambridge: Cambridge University Press

Sosa. E. (2010). *Knowing Full Well*. Princeton, NJ: Princeton University Press.

Wright, S. (2014). Sosa on knowledge from testimony. *Analysis* 74(2), 249–254.

6 A transmission theory of testimony

6.1 Introduction

Having discussed transmission, as well as internalist and reliabilist approaches to the epistemology of testimony, we are now in a position to bring the threads of the discussion together and give a theory of testimony. In the previous two chapters, I have been arguing that neither internalist nor externalist approaches to testimony can give entirely adequate accounts of testimony, since both approaches are importantly incomplete. Showing this is one thing; showing that a transmission theory can achieve the completeness that others cannot is another. In this chapter, we shall consider the contours of an approach that I believe can give an adequate account of knowledge from testimony.

The fact that the arguments against internalist and reliabilist approaches show them to be problematic because they are incomplete means that there are important insights to be had from them. In both cases, it would seem that there are cases of knowledge from testimony that they account for well. Since they do not, however, account for *all* knowledge from testimony, the theory that I propose maintains that each of the following claims about the epistemology of testimony are true:

(T1) A listener's knowledge that φ can be grounded in the speaker's transmitted epistemic grounds for φ.

(T2) A listener's knowledge that φ can be grounded in the reasons for believing the speaker's testimony that φ that the listener is aware of.

(T3) A listener's knowledge that φ can be grounded in the reliability of the processes associated with believing the speaker's testimony that φ.

At the outset, we saw that knowledge that φ is a matter of being in a certain relation to the fact that φ. The idea is that a speaker's testimony can put a listener in a position to bring about her being in this relation in various ways. Of course, a theory that allows that knowledge from testimony can be grounded in different considerations needs to account for when knowledge from testimony is grounded in each of these different ways. With this in mind, I propose the following:

(T4)   A listener's knowledge that ϕ is grounded in the speaker's transmitted grounds for ϕ only if the listener comes to know that ϕ through an epistemic assumption.

(T5)   A listener's knowledge that ϕ is grounded in the reasons for believing the speaker's testimony that ϕ only if the listener comes to know that ϕ by inferring the truth of ϕ from the fact that the speaker said that ϕ.

(T6)   A listener's knowledge that ϕ is grounded in the reliability of the processes associated with believing the speaker's testimony that ϕ only if the listener comes to know that ϕ through an assumption of reliability.[1]

We have already seen some of the considerations that motivate this view. In the rest of this chapter, I shall develop the contours of the theory further.

6.2   Transmission and the epistemology of testimony

Like the dualist approaches advanced by Paul Faulkner (2011) and Jennifer Lackey (2008), the theory that I propose attempts to reconcile the insights from various competing approaches into a single unified theory. But the theory that I propose seeks to do this in a different way to dualist theories. Where dualist theories seek to bring together internalist and externalist insights, the theory that I propose seeks to do so by suggesting the knowledge from testimony can be grounded in different ways. As a result, the theory that I propose avoids the problem for dualist approaches that was discussed in Chapter 3.

The theory that I propose makes heavy use of the idea of an assumption. With this in mind, it is worth considering further what the idea of an assumption amounts to. In §5.4, I suggested that to believe what a speaker says through an assumption – for example, the assumption that the speaker knows what she says – is to believe what the speaker says for the reason that the speaker knows what she says. In a case where the speaker does not know what she says, the fact that the speaker knows what she says cannot be the reason why the listener believes what she says, for there is no such fact. In this case, the reason why the listener believes what the speaker says is the fact that she believes that the speaker knows what she says. Yet, in a situation where the speaker does know what she says, the fact that she knows what she says becomes the reason why the listener believes what the speaker says.

A discussion from Linda Zagzebski (2012) is helpful at this juncture. Zagzebski considers a case in which someone driving a car stops at a red light because this is what the law requires – in the vocabulary we have been using here, the fact that this is what the law requires is the reason why she stops. According to Zagzebski:

> If I stop at a red light because that is what the law requires, I let the fact that the law requires it be my reason for stopping. I do not ignore the fact that I would prefer not to stop because I am in a hurry, or that I believe it is generally safer to stop, or that I do not want to take the chance of getting a high-priced traffic citation. But if I stop because the law says to do so, that reason has the status of being my reason for stopping. It can be the reason even though I am quite capable of reciting many reasons for and against stopping.
>
> (Zagzebski 2012, p. 113)

Where someone stops at a red light because this is what the law requires, the fact that this is what the law requires becomes her reason for stopping – the reason why she stops. Other reasons for stopping that she is aware of are not, in this sense, her reasons for stopping. She might be aware of various reasons for stopping and indeed aware of various reasons against stopping, but her reason for stopping, or the reason why she stops, is the fact that the law requires it.

Zagzebski also points out that stopping at a red light because this is what the law requires does not entail that she deliberately and consciously reasons that the fact that the law requires that she stop is a reason for her to stop and then acts on the basis of this reasoning. Rather, according to Zagzebski, 'rationality is doing reflectively what we do automatically and sometimes unconsciously when we adjust states of the self to resolve dissonance' (Zagzebski 2012, p. 113). In our vocabulary, this amounts to stopping on the assumption that this is what the law says. In the same way, believing what a speaker says through an assumption that she is knowledgeable does not involve explicitly considering reasons for thinking that the speaker knows what she says and coming to believe as a result of this deliberation. Rather, the assumption can be automatic and unconscious.[2]

This much may be fine, but why should anyone accept the view that a listener forming her belief through an epistemic assumption is a necessary condition of her knowledge being grounded in the speaker's transmitted epistemic grounds? In §5.4, I claimed that the best way for reliabilist approaches to account for the differences between cases in which a listener's knowledge is grounded in the reliability of the processes involved in the production of the speaker's testimony and cases in which it is grounded in the reliability of her comprehension processes is to use the idea of assumptions, but why is this the case? Giving an answer to this is crucial to the viability of the theory that I propose. With this in mind, let us consider an answer.

Elizabeth Fricker's (2015) discussion is instructive here. According to Fricker, the speech act of telling is regulated by a norm stating that one must tell someone that φ only if one knows that φ and, taking a speaker's testimony at face value when she tells a listener that φ involves the listener taking it that the speaker's testimony is what it purports to be – an expression of her knowledge that φ. This, we might think, amounts to an epistemic assumption. In a case where the speaker tells a listener that φ without knowing that φ and the listener comes to believe that φ by taking her testimony at face value, the listener intuitively does not come to know. The reason for this is straightforward. The listener assumes that the speaker knows that φ, but she does not. The listener is thus rationally committed to a falsehood. As Fricker puts it, this kind of situation 'may produce blameless belief in a justifiedly trusting recipient, and perhaps justified belief; but never knowledge' (Fricker 2015, p. 176).

This idea seems to be fundamentally correct. But if this idea is correct, then in a case where the listener forms her belief through the assumption that the speaker knows what she says, her knowledge cannot be grounded in the reliability of a set of processes – for example, the reliability of the processes involved in the production of the speaker's testimony. If the speaker failing to know what she says entails that the listener does not know what she says in a case where the listener believes what the speaker says through the assumption that the speaker is knowledgeable, then nothing grounds the listener's knowledge in such a case, for there is no such knowledge to ground. Likewise, in a case where the listener believes what the speaker says through an assumption that her testimony is reliably produced, if the speaker's testimony is not reliably produced, then the listener is rationally committed to a falsehood and thus does not come to know, regardless of whether or not the speaker's testimony expresses knowledge.

The reason that the listener is rationally committed to a falsehood in such a situation is not because the fact that the speaker's testimony being unreliably produced entails that what the speaker says is false. Rather, it is because the listener, in assuming that the speaker's testimony is reliably produced, is rationally committed to the proposition that the speaker's testimony is reliably produced. And the fact that it is not leaves the listener rationally committed to a falsehood.

One might think that the theory I propose is somewhat schizophrenic. The prospects for reconciling the insights from internalist and reliabilist approaches to testimony might seem slim, given that they are the product of fundamentally different approaches to knowledge and epistemic grounds. The internalist idea and the reliabilist idea of what kind of relationship to a fact constitutes knowledge are drastically different, so one might think that the prospects for reconciliation are slim. Nonetheless, there is supposed to be a single unified idea behind the theory that I propose. It is the reliabilist idea – that epistemic grounds are that which secure the modal profile of the belief. Whilst I have no particular view as to whether the relevant modal profile should be understood in terms of reliability, safety or sensitivity, this is the guiding idea behind the theory that I propose.

Guided by this idea, we can see that the theory that I propose is apt to return the intuitively correct verdicts in the circular testimony cases involved in the argument against internalist approaches to testimony that I presented in §4.4. Unlike internalist approaches to testimony, the theory I propose is able to distinguish between cases of circular testimony in which the original speaker's epistemic grounds are enhanced and cases in which they are not. In the case where the original speaker's epistemic grounds are not enhanced, it is intuitive that the reason for this is the fact that the testimonial situation is circular in a particular way. By contrast, in cases where the original speaker's epistemic grounds are enhanced, the idea is that this is possible because there is an important difference between the circularity in that situation and the situation where the original speaker's epistemic grounds are not enhanced. Since the theory I propose rejects the internalist idea that the fact that the cases are subjectively indistinguishable entails that there is no difference with respect to epistemic grounds, the theory that I propose can give the intuitively correct account.

6.3   Assurances and evidence

One issue that has come to prominence in the epistemology of testimony is the question of whether or not the epistemology of testimony should be guided by the idea that testimony constitutes evidence of what is said. Traditionally, the basic idea behind the epistemology of testimony is that speakers produce statements and these statements constitute evidence of the truth of what they say. This evidence, in the right circumstances, grounds the listener's knowledge of the truth of what is said. Of course, ideas about what the right circumstances might be vary, but the general idea nonetheless remains constant.

More recently, however, dissenting voices have emerged against this picture.[3] Rather than thinking of testimony as constituting evidence of what is said, epistemologists have focused on the idea of a speaker's act of testifying as presenting an *assurance*. As Edward Hinchman points out, in presenting an assurance 'the speaker assures [the listener] not merely that it is true that *p* but that this very assurance entitles [the listener] to close deliberation and believe that *p*' (Hinchman 2014, p. 14). This is important. The idea is that, in telling a listener that things are thus and so, the speaker assures the listener not merely that things are thus and so but also that the listener need carry her own investigation no further and can simply believe that things are thus and so.

The central difference between evidence and assurance is that, where something's status as evidence is typically undermined by the observation that it was produced deliberately and voluntarily with the intention of eliciting belief, something's status as an assurance *depends* on it being produced in this way. Moran points out that finding out that something taken to be evidence was in fact produced deliberately and voluntarily brings us to disregard it as evidence, whereas something produced involuntarily does not qualify as an assurance, in much the same way that talking in one's sleep is not a way of making a promise (Moran 2005, pp. 6–7). The observation that testimonial situations, at least in cases in which a speaker tells a listener something, anyway, have distinctively interpersonal dimensions.[4]

Naturally, there is substantial dissent to the idea that the epistemology of testimony should be organised around the concept of assurance rather than that of evidence.[5] One might think that the theory proposed entails nothing about the dispute over evidence-based approaches against assurance-based approaches to testimony. It is natural to think that settling this dispute shows us the details of the theory of testimony that I propose should be spelled out, but that the theory itself is neutral with respect to which account is correct. This, however, is mistaken. The theory I propose does give us an indication of what we should think about the dispute over how to approach the epistemology of testimony. As we shall see, according to the theory of testimony that I propose, making adequate sense of testimony as an epistemic source involves employing *both* the idea of testimony as evidence *and* the idea that testimony can ground knowledge through the presentation of assurance.

This is not to say that any particular case of knowledge must be explained both in terms of testimony constituting evidence and a presented assurance. Assurance theorists correctly regard these as incompatible. This does not, however, entail that each notion might be dispensable to accounting for different cases to give a complete epistemology of testimony. The central idea is that the question of whether an instance of knowledge from testimony is to be explained in terms of evidence or through the presentation of an assurance depends on how the speaker's testimony is produced. If the speaker's testimony is produced deliberately and voluntarily, in the way associated with telling, then the listener's acquired knowledge is to be explained in terms of a presented assurance. By contrast, if the speaker's testimony is not produced in this way, then the listener's knowledge is to be explained in terms of the speaker's testimony constituting evidence. The theory thus proposes to reconcile the insights from these two positions as well as the insights from the internalist and reliabilist positions.

As with the previous attempt at reconciliation, the idea is that different views account for different cases. In §2.3 I developed a conception of epistemic sincerity according to which a speaker's testimony is epistemically sincere if and only if the reason why she says that φ is because of someone's epistemic grounds for φ. I also pointed out in §2.5 that someone's testimony might be epistemically sincere for a number of reasons. One is that the speaker considers her epistemic grounds and what they best support and consciously decides to tell the listener that φ because this is what someone's epistemic grounds speak in favour of. Another is a case in which the possibility of saying anything other than what her epistemic grounds best support never enters the speaker's head. A third involves the speaker taking a truth serum that makes her say whatever her epistemic grounds best support. Epistemic sincerity can be brought about in various different ways, and in order to account for all them, we need both the notion of evidence and the notion of assurance.

In cases where the speaker's testimony is produced deliberately and voluntarily, with the intention of eliciting a belief in a listener, explaining the transmission of knowledge in terms of the speaker's testimony constituting evidence is problematic, for the reasons that assurance theorists such as Moran give. Since not all epistemically sincere testimony is produced in the way associated with telling, not all instances of knowledge transmission can be accounted for in terms of assurance. In cases where the epistemic sincerity of the speaker's testimony is to be explained in terms other than the speaker producing testimony in this way – for example, in a case where a speaker has taken a truth serum that compels her to say what her epistemic grounds best support – the speaker's testimony does not have the character associated with assurance and thus needs to be explained in terms of evidence.

Since the view that I propose maintains that thinking of the epistemology of testimony in terms of assurances is fundamentally correct, at least in some cases, it is important to consider the case against assurance-based approaches. I believe that the challenges in the literature can be met, but it is worth first calling attention to one possible confusion to be avoided. One might think that, if we think about assurances as providing epistemic grounds, then there will inevitably be an asymmetry between the speaker's epistemic grounds and the listener's, even in cases that are ostensibly to be explained in terms of transmission. For the listener's knowledge will be grounded in the speaker's presented assurance, but the speaker's presented assurance does not ground her knowledge.

Rather than thinking of assurances as a reason that grounds knowledge from testimony, I believe that we should think of assurances as a mechanism by which epistemic grounds are transmitted.[6] The same is true of the idea of testimony as evidence.[7] A similar asymmetry might seem to emerge with the observation that the listener's knowledge will be grounded in the evidence constituted by the speaker's testimony, but the speaker's knowledge is not grounded in this evidence. Again, this problem is avoided by the idea that the evidence constituted by testimony does not provide an epistemic ground of its own but serves as the mechanism by which the speaker's testimony makes her epistemic grounds available to the listener.

With this point in hand, let us turn to consider two other objections. Jennifer Lackey (2008) objects that, even if approaching testimony through the idea that testimony constitutes evidence of what is said makes for an odd account of the interpersonal dynamics of the conversion, there is no *epistemic* problem with this. Whilst a listener treating a speaker's testimony as evidence might be problematic at a psychological or at a moral level, there is no epistemic problem. And in the absence of an epistemic problem, we ought not to discard the idea that testimony constitutes evidence of what is said (Lackey 2008, p. 249). However, according to the theory that I propose, an epistemic problem is not far to seek.

Suppose that I see a clock saying that the time is 11:51. I might ordinarily think that the clock is operating in the usual way without interference, but if I subsequently learn that it was manipulated by Alison to make me think that the time is 11:51, as Moran points out, I come to regard it differently. I need not discount it as an epistemic source – perhaps I think that Alison set it to that time knowing when I would be passing and wanting to inform me – but I do come to think of it differently to when I previously took it to be functioning normally. If I continue to regard it as a clock that is functioning normally, whilst knowing that it is not, my knowledge that it is not functions as a defeater for the beliefs that I form in this way.

This brings us to the answer to Lackey's question. The problem with treating testimony as evidence is that it involves treating it as something that is not deliberately and voluntarily produced whilst knowing that it is. Forming a belief in what someone says on the basis that it is not produced in this way whilst knowing that it is means that one immediately has a defeater for one's belief. Also, the idea that someone's epistemic grounds are already defeated in virtue of the way that she forms her belief *is* an epistemic problem with treating testimony as evidence. This is true whether the listener forms her belief through an inference, using the idea of the speaker's testimony as evidence as a premise in her reasoning, or through an assumption that this is the case.

Another objection to assurance approaches to testimony is given by Arnon Keren (2012). Against Moran's point about discovering that something taken to be evidence was in fact produced deliberately and voluntarily, Keren notes that this discovery does not always undermine the evidential status of the thing taken to be evidence. In the case where Herod presents Salome with the severed head of John the Baptist, the act is deliberate, voluntary and intended to elicit the relevant belief. Furthermore, Salome recognises it as such, but this – rightly – does not undermine the evidential status of John's head for her (Keren 2012, p. 703). Keren's point here is well-made, but there are two points that can be brought to bear in defence of assurance approaches.

First, the case that Keren describes is not an instance of telling but an instance of *deliberately and openly letting know*. Indeed, it is the example of deliberately and openly letting know that Moran discusses.[8] The result is that, even if the discovery that something was deliberately and intentionally produced does not always undermine its evidential status, the case here does not show that it does not do so in cases of telling.

Second, consider again the idea that discovering that the clock I see was in fact set in order for me to see it. In such a situation, it need not be the case that I abandon the idea that I can believe on the basis of its deliverances, but it is the case that I come to regard it differently. My doing so, however, is consistent with my continuing to regard it as an epistemic source, albeit one that is an epistemic source in virtue of the fact that an assurance is being presented.

The theory that I propose is thus not neutral between assurance-based approaches and evidence-based approaches. It is a version of an assurance theory, albeit with one that gives a role to the presented assurance that is not the one traditionally suggested by those who endorse assurance theories. This is not to say that the concept of evidence is irrelevant to the epistemology of testimony, or that all instances of testimony are to be thought of in terms of assurances. I am doubtful as to whether any advocates of assurance theories of testimony have ever thought that, but it is to say that the theory that I propose entails that the idea of assurances is indispensable to an adequate account of how testimony transmits knowledge and epistemic grounds.

6.4 Entitlements and obligations

We can thus see that the theory that I propose has implications for the question of whether the epistemology of testimony should be approached through the idea of *evidence* or *assurance*. As we saw in Chapter 3, it also has implications for the question of whether or not a listener can acquire knowledge and epistemic grounds through testimony only if she is aware of reasons for believing what the speaker says. One point that the theory that I propose remains neutral on, however, is the nature of the entitlement to believe what speakers say. Specifically, it is compatible with the view that listeners have an entitlement to believe what they are told unless they are aware of countervailing reasons in cases where the speaker's testimony does not make knowledge or epistemic grounds available to the listener. Furthermore, it is compatible with either the idea that listeners have a right to believe what a speaker says in the absence of reasons against doing so, or an obligation to do so.

Like the kind of entitlement theories advanced by Tyler Burge (1993, 1997), Edward Hinchman (2005, 2013, 2014) and Axel Gelfert (2010, 2014), the theory that I propose maintains that a listener can come to acquire knowledge and epistemic grounds through testimony even if she is not aware of reasons for believing the speaker's testimony. In other words, in at least some cases where a speaker's testimony makes knowledge and epistemic grounds available to a listener, the listener believing what the speaker says in the absence of reasons for doing so is unproblematic. Moreover, according to these theories, the listener's entitlement to believe what the speaker says does not have anything to do with the speaker's epistemic position with respect to what she says. In other words, a listener who is told something by a speaker who has no reason for believing the truth of what she says can have just the same entitlement as a listener who is told something by a speaker who says something because she knows it.

Burge, for example, maintains that a listener's entitlement to believe what a speaker says is underpinned by a series of entitlements. One is the entitlement to assume that something that appears to be presented as true is in fact presented as true. Another is the entitlement to assume that what seems to be intelligible is in fact intelligible. A third is the entitlement to assume that what is intelligible is presented by a rational source. Finally, a fourth is the entitlement to assume that what is presented by a rational source is in fact true (Burge 1993, p. 469). Taken together, these add up to an entitlement to believe what seems to be an instance of testimony. These entitlements are grounded *a priori*. As such, there is nothing in the grounds of the entitlement to believe testimony that applies in cases where a speaker's testimony makes knowledge and epistemic grounds available, but not in cases where it does not.

Equally, Hinchman argues that a listener's entitlement to believe what a speaker says comes from the speaker's presented assurance or invitation to trust the speaker. According to Hinchman, the presentation of an invitation to trust makes an entitlement available to a listener.[9] Of course, whether or not the presented invitation puts the listener in a position to know depends on the speaker's epistemic position. But the presentation of an invitation to trust is constitutive of the speech act of telling, according to Hinchman's view. As such, a listener has an epistemic entitlement to believe what a speaker says in the absence of reasons against doing so, and this is so both in cases where the speaker's testimony makes knowledge available and in cases in which it does not.

By contrast, John McDowell's (1994) disjunctivist approach to testimony gives the clearest example of a theory that maintains that there is an entitlement available to a listener in cases where the speaker's testimony makes knowledge available that is not available to her in cases where the speaker's testimony does not. McDowell explicitly states that, in a paradigm case of a tourist coming to know the whereabouts of the cathedral through testimony, 'I think that the tourist is entitled to her belief about where the cathedral is [. . .] but I do not think that this is because he is exercising a general presumption of sincerity and competence' (McDowell 1994, p. 218, n. 211). According to McDowell, in cases where a speaker's testimony does not make knowledge available to the listener, the listener does not have the same entitlement to believe what the speaker says.[10]

The theory that I propose insists that, at least sometimes, in a case where a speaker's testimony makes knowledge and epistemic grounds available, the listener believing what the speaker says without being aware of reasons for doing so is epistemically unproblematic. This might be explained in terms of the listener having an entitlement to believe testimony that covers *both* cases in which a speaker's testimony makes knowledge and epistemic grounds available *and* cases in which it does not, or it might be explained in terms of an entitlement *only* in cases in which the speaker's testimony makes knowledge and epistemic grounds available. More accurately, it might be explained in terms of believing what a speaker says without being aware of reasons for doing so being unproblematic only in a *proper subset* of cases in which the speaker's testimony makes knowledge and epistemic grounds available. The theory that I propose is neutral with respect to these claims.

Furthermore, the theory that I propose is neutral with respect to the question of whether listeners, in cases where they can acquire knowledge and epistemic grounds by believing the speaker's testimony without reasons for doing so, have an *obligation* to believe the speaker's testimony in the absence of countervailing reasons, or merely a *right* to do so. Insofar as the entitlements that Burge, Hinchman and McDowell identify have rational force, one might think that they make someone rationally obliged to believe what a speaker says in the absence of reasons against doing so. Hinchman suggests that to not believe a speaker's testimony in the absence of reasons for doing so is to *slight* the speaker (Hinchman 2005, p. 565). This, however, is an interpersonal matter between the speaker and the listener. The question is whether or not the listener, in not believing the speaker in the absence of reasons for doing so, does something that she is rationally obliged not to do.

The clearest statement of the view that, in the absence of reasons against doing so, a listener is obliged to believe what a speaker says is given by Axel Gelfert (2014). As we saw in §3.3, Gelfert argues that a listener's right to believe what a speaker says without being aware of reasons for doing so is grounded in a prior inference concerning the reliability of testimony. According to Gelfert, the effect of this inference 'is that of justifying a stance of default acceptance, whereas rejection of testimony requires special reasons that override the hearer's default justification to accept what she is told' (Gelfert 2014, p. 140). The result is that, according to Gelfert, not only is a listener allowed to believe what a speaker says in the absence of reasons against doing so, she is rationally required to do so.

Unlike Gelfert's theory – and plausibly other entitlement theories as well – the theory that I propose is neutral with respect to the question of whether a listener merely has a right to believe what a speaker says in the absence of reasons against doing so, or has an obligation to do so. The theory that I propose entails that it must be at least permissible for a listener to believe what a speaker says without being aware of reasons for doing so, but it is neutral with respect to the question of whether or not a listener violates a rational obligation in not believing in such cases.

6.5   Conclusion

The purpose of this chapter has been to bring together the threads from the foregoing discussion and to develop and clarify the theory of testimony that I believe can unify the insights from the competing traditions discussed earlier. Knowledge, as we have been thinking about it, is a matter of standing in a certain relation to a fact. The theory that I propose maintains that this relationship can be grounded in various ways. It can be grounded in reasons for believing the speaker's testimony that the listener is aware of, or in reliable processes, or in the transmission of knowledge and epistemic grounds. Each is individually indispensable and together they give what I take to be a viable epistemology of testimony.

The resulting theory maintains that what grounds knowledge from testimony depends on the way in which the listener forms her belief. If she forms her belief through an assumption of reliability – for example, the assumption that her comprehension processes are reliable – then her knowledge from testimony can only be grounded in the reliability of her comprehension processes. Explaining how testimony functions as a source of knowledge requires both the idea that telling someone that things are a certain way involves the presentation of an assurance and the idea that a speaker's testimony can constitute evidence of what she says. Lastly, I have argued that whilst the theory needs to allow that a listener believing a speaker's testimony without being aware of reasons for doing so is unproblematic, at least in some cases where a speaker's testimony makes knowledge and epistemic grounds available, it is compatible with a variety of positions regarding the question of whether or not a listener is obliged to believe what the speaker says in such situations and whether or not the listener's entitlement also extends to cases in which a speaker's testimony does not make knowledge and epistemic grounds available.

Notes

1 As with the assumption that the speaker knows what she says, the assumption of reliability gives rise to knowledge only if it is true. Otherwise, the case is (at best) an instance of justified true belief that does not constitute knowledge for the reasons described in Chapter 2.
2 In much the same way, I pointed out in §2.5 that a speaker's testimony being epistemically sincere does not entail that she consciously decides to say what her epistemic grounds best support.
3 The case against testimony as evidence is led by Angus Ross (1986). More recently, the case has been forcefully picked up by Richard Moran (2005), Edward Hinchman (2005), Paul Faulkner (2011) and Benjamin McMyler (2011).
4 Sanford Goldberg (2015) argues that these interpersonal dimensions can be accounted for more effectively through the idea that the speech act of telling is governed by a norm stating that one must assert only what one knows.
5 See Jennifer Lackey (2008) and Arnon Keren (2012).
6 The line I am presenting here is how I propose to respond to the dilemma for assurance-based approaches that Jennifer Lackey (2008) presents.
7 This is similar to the view endorsed by Edward Hinchman (2014) according to which a speaker's testimony that φ making the kind of entitlement that permits the listener to close her investigation into φ depends on the speaker meeting the responsibilities associated with telling the listener that φ, understood as having sufficient epistemic grounds for φ that would allow the listener to close her investigation. In a case where the speaker does not have such epistemic grounds, her assurance does not make such an entitlement available to the listener (Hinchman 2014, p. 16).
8 The idea of deliberately and openly letting know is from H.P. Grice (1989).
9 Goldberg (2015) argues against the idea that interpersonal features of testimony can ground a distinctively epistemic entitlement.
10 McDowell's notion of entitlement differs substantially from the notion of entitlement offered by Burge and other entitlement theorists. Most notably, McDowell's use of an entitlement appears to be such that the only cases in

which someone is entitled to her belief are cases in which she is also aware of reasons for it. Furthermore, the entitlement appears to consist entirely in the reasons that she is aware of. See also McDowell (2002).

Bibliography

Burge, T. (1993). Content preservation. *Philosophical Review* 102(4), 457–488.

Burge, T. (1997). Interlocution, perception, and memory. *Philosophical Studies* 86(1), 21–47.

Faulkner, P. (2011). *Knowledge on Trust*. Oxford: Oxford University Press.

Fricker, E. (2015). How to make invidious distinctions amongst reliable testifiers. *Episteme* 12(2), 173–202.

Gelfert, A. (2010). Reconsidering the role of inference to the best explanation in the epistemology of testimony. *Studies in History and Philosophy of Science* 41(4), 386–396.

Gelfert, A. (2014). *A Critical Introduction to Testimony*. London: Bloomsbury.

Goldberg, S. (2015). *Assertion: On the Philosophical Significance of Assertoric Speech*. Oxford: Oxford University Press.

Grice, H.P. (1989). *Studies in the Way of Words*. Cambridge MA: Harvard University Press.

Hinchman, E. (2005). Telling as inviting to trust. *Philosophy and Phenomenological Research* 70(3), 562–587.

Hinchman, E. (2013). Assertion, sincerity, and knowledge. *Noûs* 47(4), 613–646.

Hinchman, E. (2014). Assurance and warrant. *Philosophers' Imprint* 14(17), 1–58.

Keren, A. (2012). On the alleged perversity of the evidential view of testimony. *Analysis* 72(4), 700–707.

Lackey, J. (2008). *Learning from Words*. Oxford: Oxford University Press.

McDowell, J. (1994). Knowledge by hearsay. In B. Matilal and A. Chakrabarti (Eds.), *Knowing from Words*, pp. 195–224. Dordrecht: Kluwer Academic Publishers.

McDowell, J. (2002). Knowledge and the internal revisited. *Philosophy and Phenomenological Research* 64(1), 97–105.

McMyler, B. (2011). *Testimony, Trust, and Authority*. Oxford: Oxford University Press.

Moran, R. (2005). Getting told and being believed. *Philosophers' Imprint* 5, 1–29.

Ross, A. (1986). Why do we believe what we are told? *Ratio* 28(1), 69–88.

Zagzebski, L. T. (2012). *Epistemic Authority: A Theory of Trust, Authority, and Autonomy in Belief*. Oxford: Oxford University Press.

7 Objections to transmission

7.1 Introduction

Having seen the way that I believe the notion of transmission should be developed into an epistemological theory of testimony, we can turn to consider some of the various influential objections that have been made against transmission theories in the philosophical literature. Primarily, these have been based on counterexamples, which purport to show that transmission theories are committed to implausible claims about certain types of testimonial situation. Some purport to show that the notion of transmission is dispensable to the epistemology of testimony, others purport to show that thinking of the epistemology of testimony in terms of transmission is outright mistaken. I believe, however, that each of the objections can be met.

In this chapter, I shall discuss four prominent types of counterexample. The first are based on the idea of speakers who do not know what they say, but whose testimony can intuitively be a source of knowledge nonetheless. The second purport to show that transmission theories are incompatible with Subject-Sensitive Invariantism about knowledge ascriptions. The third are based on cases in which speakers do not know what they say because their beliefs lack the relevant epistemic grounds. Finally, the fourth are based on the idea that beliefs based on testimony can be safe in cases where neither the speaker's belief nor the speaker's testimony is safe. Each case is supposed to be difficult for transmission theorists to account for, but I shall argue that none of these cases undermines the transmission theory that I propose.

7.2 The creationist schoolteacher objection

Cases in which speakers who do not know what they say, but can nonetheless intuitively put listeners in a position to know the truth of what they say, are one of the most prominent objections to transmission approaches to testimony. Jennifer Lackey's (2008) case has been particularly influential in this regard. In Lackey's version of the case, a schoolteacher of creationist sympathies tells her class propositions about evolution. The speaker does not believe the propositions she tells her class, but she nonetheless realises that the scientific evidence overwhelmingly supports them and that her own creationist beliefs are based on nothing more than faith. Mindful of her obligation to tell her class what the evidence best supports, the teacher tells her students the propositions about evolution (Lackey 2008, p. 48).

This gives rise to the following argument:

(28) The listeners can come to know what the speaker says by believing her testimony.

(29) If the knowledge that the listeners acquire by believing the speaker's testimony cannot be accounted for in terms of transmission, then transmission theories are false.

(30) The knowledge the listeners acquire by believing the speaker's testimony cannot be accounted for in terms of transmission.

Therefore

(31) Transmission theories are false.

By and large, **(28)** seems to be uncontroversial. One notable dissenter is Robert Audi (2006), who suggests that the fact that the speaker's testimony is doxastically insincere undermines the idea that the listeners can come to know what the speaker says by believing her testimony. Audi also points out that, if the school had required her to say something false, the speaker would have done so (Audi 2006, p. 29). One might object to this claim on two grounds. First, as we shall see, doxastic insincerity does not entail unreliability. A speaker's testimony can, in certain situations, be reliable *exactly because* it is doxastically insincere. Second, even if doxastic insincerity does entail unreliability, a speaker's testimony being reliable is not a necessary condition of it being a source of knowledge. As we saw in §2.3, a speaker's testimony might be epistemically sincere without being reliable, and insofar as it is epistemically sincere it can make knowledge available to the listeners.

I therefore believe that transmission theorists would be ill-advised to resist **(28)**. The case for **(29)** is interesting, though. One might think that transmission theorists need not account for the knowledge made available in terms of transmission. For example, the view that I propose allows that knowledge from testimony can be grounded in the reliability of the processes involved in the production of the speaker's testimony. One might wonder why transmission theories such as the one that I propose are obliged to account for the knowledge available to the listeners in this case in terms of transmission. The point can be secured, however, by adjusting **(28)** to the following:

(28*) The listeners can come to know what the speaker says by believing her testimony through an epistemic assumption.

One might think that this does not undermine the intuitive force of **(28)**, but given the discussion in §6.2, this instead means that the knowledge available to the listeners must be accounted for in terms of transmission, as **(29)** states.

By far the most controversial premise in the argument is **(30)**. Transmission theorists typically reject **(30)**. Paul Faulkner (2011) argues that the knowledge available to the listeners can be explained in terms of transmission. The idea is that, rather than being transmitted from the speaker, it is transmitted from the sources upon which the speaker depends – the scientists responsible for uncovering the facts that the speaker reports (Faulkner 2011, p. 61). Tyler Burge (2013) rejects **(30)** and the argument against transmission on similar grounds. As Burge puts it, 'they fail because they do not take account of the provision that the source of knowledge in the antecedent chain need not be the recipient's immediate interlocutor' (Burge 2013, p. 256).

This line of response, however, can be avoided by a modified version of the case. In this spirit, Peter Graham (2006) considers a case in which the speaker herself finds a fossil that nobody has seen before and infers that dinosaurs used to be in the place she is standing millions of years ago. Nobody else knows this because nobody else has seen the fossil, and the speaker does not know it because she does not believe it. The result is that the knowledge made available to the listeners cannot be explained in terms of transmission. The argument against transmission theories might thus be developed on the basis of this case.[1]

Nonetheless, the argument can be resisted by denying **(30)**. Whilst the creationist schoolteacher cases cannot be characterised in terms of the transmission of knowledge, they can be characterised in terms of the transmission of epistemic grounds. In each case, the speaker has epistemic grounds for what she says, and it is these epistemic grounds that come to underpin the listener's knowledge. And as we have seen in various places, primarily in the initial statements of the transmission of knowledge and epistemic grounds given in Chapter 1, the transmission of epistemic grounds is the more fundamental notion. The result is that, whilst the cases cannot be characterised in terms of the transmission of knowledge, they can be characterised in the transmission of epistemic grounds.

In terms of the above argument, this means that there is a fallacy of ambiguity. Specifically, **(30)** is ambiguous between the following two claims:

(30*)   The knowledge the listeners acquire by believing the speaker's testimony cannot be accounted for in terms of the transmission of knowledge.

(30**) The knowledge the listeners acquire by believing the speaker's testimony cannot be accounted for in terms of the transmission of epistemic grounds.

The claim in **(30*)** is true, but it is unproblematic for transmission theories. Even if the knowledge the listeners acquire cannot be accounted for in terms of the transmission of knowledge, it does not follow that it cannot be accounted for in terms of transmission *simpliciter*. The claim in **(30**)** would be problematic for transmission theories if it were true, but it is not.

Those who think of epistemic grounds in terms of justification are apt to distinguish between *doxastic* justification and *propositional* justification. The former is justification that supports beliefs; the latter is justification that does not, either because the subject does not have the relevant belief, or because her belief is not connected in the right way to – that is to say, is not based on – her justification. In the same way, those who differentiate between justification and epistemic grounds might also seek to distinguish between having doxastic epistemic grounds and having propositional epistemic grounds. Doing so allows us to characterise the creationist schoolteacher cases in terms of the transmission of epistemic grounds.

In the creationist schoolteacher cases, the speaker's epistemic grounds – in the form of propositional epistemic grounds – become the listener's epistemic grounds. Since the listener believes what the speaker says through an epistemic assumption, her belief is based on these epistemic grounds, and they thus become doxastic epistemic grounds for her. This accounts for why the listener intuitively comes to know what the speaker says through an epistemic assumption.[2] It does so by characterising the cases in terms of transmission in the most fundamental sense. The result is that the cases based on creationist schoolteachers do not undermine transmission theories.

7.3   SSI and undefeated defeater objections

A second case against transmission is built around the idea that transmission in the epistemology of testimony is incompatible with Subject-Sensitive Invariantism (SSI) about knowledge ascriptions. The central idea behind SSI is that the question of whether or not someone knows that ϕ is not simply a function of the truth of her belief and the epistemic grounds that support it. Rather, advocates of SSI maintain that the question of whether or not someone knows that ϕ depends on the epistemic standards that are relevant to her. Exactly which standards are relevant depends, in John Hawthorne's words, on 'the attention, interests, and stakes of that subject at the time' (Hawthorne 2004, p. 158).[3] In other words, advocates of SSI maintain that someone's ability to be guided by the fact that ϕ depends on non-epistemic factors, such as what is at stake for her with respect to ϕ.

There is undoubtedly some intuitive plausibility to SSI. If I am highly allergic to nuts but you are not, it seems that you might be able to know that the brownie does not contain nuts just by looking at it, whereas I need to investigate further. This can be explained in terms of the idea that it matters much more to me whether or not there are nuts in the brownie, meaning that the standards relevant to me knowing are higher than the standards relevant to you knowing. According to Jennifer Lackey (2008) and John MacFarlane (2005), however, this intuitive insight is at odds with transmission theories of testimony.

Lackey's case involves a speaker who is familiar with the local geography telling a listener the whereabouts of the nearest coffee shop. The speaker does not know what she says because she is subject to unusually high epistemic standards. The listener, however, is subject to substantially lower standards (Lackey 2008, p. 61). The result is the following argument:

(32) The listener can come to know what the speaker says by believing her testimony.
(33) If the listener's knowledge cannot be explained in terms of transmission, then transmission theories are false.
(34) The listener's knowledge cannot be explained in terms of transmission.

Therefore

(35) Transmission theories are false.

John MacFarlane's case is different. In MacFarlane's case, a speaker tells a listener that their car is on the drive. The speaker knows this and the listener comes to know it by believing what she says. The stakes are then raised for the speaker, but not the listener, and the original speaker asks the listener whether or not the car is still on the drive. The listener, with no further grounds for thinking this, tells the speaker that it is (MacFarlane 2005, p. 34). This gives rise to the following argument:

(36) The original speaker cannot come to know what the original listener says by believing her testimony.

(37)   If the original speaker cannot come to know what the original listener says by believing her testimony, then transmission theories are false.

Therefore

(38)   Transmission theories are false.

The arguments clearly have a lot in common. Both depend on SSI. In Lackey's case, those who endorse SSI should allow that the listener can come to know what the speaker says by believing her testimony – as **(32)** states – because the standards for her knowing are sufficiently low. In MacFarlane's case, those who endorse SSI should allow that the listener cannot come to know what the speaker says by believing her testimony – as **(36)** states – because the standards for her knowing are sufficiently high.

In each case, however, the SSI characterisation appears incompatible with the characterisation transmission theorists seem committed to. Suppose that the listener in Lackey's case believes what the speaker says through an epistemic assumption. This establishes **(33)**. But the listener's knowledge cannot be explained in terms of transmission because the speaker does not know what she says (and we can stipulate that nobody else does either). This establishes **(34)**. In MacFarlane's case, the speaker does know what she says, so in the right conditions (which can be stipulated to obtain) the speaker should be able to transmit her knowledge to the listener. This is the idea behind **(37)**. The fact that she intuitively cannot is problematic for transmission theorists.

It is worth noting that the intuition in MacFarlane's case is the same intuition that I exploited in the argument against internalist approaches in §4.4. MacFarlane's idea is that a speaker cannot improve her epistemic position simply by cycling her belief through listeners who have no independent grounds for what she says (MacFarlane 2005, p. 134). This is just what takes place when the speaker tells the listener that their car is on the drive and the listener subsequently tells the original speaker this. This is just the same intuition that was behind the argument against internalist approaches to testimony in §4.4 – and yet here it is being used to underpin an argument against transmission theories. MacFarlane's argument thus shows that the intuition here is not distinctive to transmission theorists. Rather, it is something that one should find intuitive whether or not one ultimately endorses a transmission approach to the epistemology of testimony.

Both of these objections, however, can be fended off in the same way as the objections based on creationist schoolteachers. Both cases can be accounted for in terms of the transmission of epistemic grounds. In Lackey's case, the idea is that the speaker's epistemic grounds are transmitted to the listener. The epistemic grounds are not sufficient to put the speaker in a position to know, since the standards associated with her knowing are unusually high. But when they are acquired by the listener, they are sufficient to put her in a position to know because the standards associated with her knowing are substantially lower. In MacFarlane's case, the same characterisation is available. The original listener has some epistemic grounds for what she says. These put her in a position to know the truth of what the speaker says because the standards associated with her knowing are sufficiently low. They are then transmitted to the original speaker, but because the standards associated with her knowing are higher, they do not put her in a position to know what the original listener says.

In each case, the characterisation that comes from the idea behind SSI is compatible with the characterisation in terms of the transmission of epistemic grounds – the more fundamental sense of transmission. In terms of the above arguments, this means that **(34)** is false because it is ambiguous between the claim that the case cannot be characterised in terms of knowledge transmission, which is true but unproblematic, and the claim that the case cannot be characterised in terms of transmission *simpliciter*, which is false. In the case of MacFarlane's argument, the claim in **(37)** is false. Transmission theories do not entail that the original listener can bring the original speaker to know what she says. Rather, they entail that the original listener can make her epistemic grounds available to the original speaker, which is exactly what happens in the case.

Now, in making this argument against transmission, Lackey insists that the factors that raise the standards for the speaker should be thought of in terms of *defeaters*. The idea is that the speaker's epistemic grounds are defeated, whereas the listener's epistemic grounds are not. A similar characterisation is available in MacFarlane's case. The result is that the cases cannot be described in terms of transmitted epistemic grounds. Where the epistemic grounds are defeated, the speaker (in Lackey's case) and the listener (in MacFarlane's case) do not merely have epistemic grounds that do not put them in a position to know. Rather, they lack epistemic grounds altogether. Transmission theorists who want to endorse SSI, however, can resist this idea. Reconciling the idea behind transmission with the idea behind SSI involves showing that there is a coherent way of maintaining both the SSI characterisation of the cases Lackey and MacFarlane give and the transmission characterisation of these cases. This can be done by maintaining that the change in standards does not constitute a defeater but constitutes a consideration that prevents the speaker (in Lackey's case) and the listener (in MacFarlane's case) from knowing what they are told.

There are, however, further cases in which it is clear that the speaker *does* lack epistemic grounds for what she says. Lackey provides two of these. In one, the speaker is systematically mistaken with respect to φ such that, whenever she sees that φ, she is disposed to believe that ~φ and is also systematically insincere such that whenever she believes that ~φ, she is disposed to say that φ. The result is that the speaker's testimony that φ is reliable (Lackey 2008, pp. 53–54). In the second case, the speaker is aware of various reasons for thinking that her visual faculties are unreliable. However, she ignores these reasons and forms the belief that ψ on the basis of the visual appearance that ψ. She then tells a listener that ψ. Unbeknownst to the speaker, her visual faculties are in fact highly reliable and the evidence against them is misleading. The result is that the speaker's testimony that ψ is, in fact, reliably produced (Lackey 2008, p. 59). Each case is taken to motivate the following argument:

(39)   The listener can come to know what the speaker says by believing her testimony.

(40)   If the listener's knowledge cannot be explained in terms of transmission, then transmission theories are false.

(41)   The listener's knowledge cannot be explained in terms of transmission.

Therefore

(42)   Transmission theories are false.

The claim in **(39)** is backed up by the observation that each speaker's testimony is reliably produced.[4] The claim in **(41)** is backed up by the observation that the speaker neither knows nor has epistemic grounds for what she says. In the case of the speaker who reliably says that φ when she sees that φ and believes that ~φ, she has no grounds for φ because she believes that ~φ. In the case of the speaker who says that ψ, her epistemic grounds for ψ are defeated by the reasons that she is aware of for thinking that her visual capacities are unreliable. Unlike the previous cases, then, there is no prospect of explaining the cases in terms of transmission, whether this is understood in terms of knowledge transmission or the transmission of epistemic grounds. The problem, however, is with the claim in **(40)**.

In order for the claim in **(40)** to be true – and applicable to the proposed transmission theory of testimony – it must be stipulated that the listener comes to know what the speaker says through an epistemic assumption. According to the theory that I propose, if the listener comes to know through an assumption of reliability, then her knowledge is grounded in the reliability of the relevant processes. The fact that the speaker neither knows nor has epistemic grounds for what she says is irrelevant. Hence, the speaker's lack of knowledge and epistemic grounds matters only if the listener forms her belief through an epistemic assumption.

We have already seen, however, the way to respond to this objection on behalf of the theory that I propose. If it is stipulated that the listener forms her belief through an epistemic assumption, then there is also reason for thinking that the listener does not come to know what the speaker says, leaving **(39)** unmotivated. In §6.2 we saw that, in a situation where the listener forms her belief through an epistemic assumption, she lets the fact that the speaker has knowledge of epistemic grounds for what she says, rather than the fact that the speaker's testimony is reliable, be her reason for believing. But in a situation where the speaker has no such knowledge or epistemic grounds, the listener's belief does not amount to knowledge.

In terms of the above argument, **(39)** rests on a stipulation that rules out **(40)**. In order for **(39)** to be plausible, it must be the case that the listener does not form her belief through an epistemic assumption. For if she does, then there are reasons for thinking that she does not come to know by believing the speaker. According to the theory that I advocate, though, this stipulation means that the listener's knowledge does not have to be explained in terms of transmission. If the listener's belief is not formed through an epistemic assumption, then the listener's knowledge is not to be explained in terms of transmission.[5]

One might be concerned that the claim that knowledge and epistemic grounds are transmitted only if a listener forms her belief through an epistemic assumption is overly restrictive. However, it is not as though the theory that I propose maintains that a listener forming her belief through an epistemic assumption is a necessary condition of the listener coming to know the truth of what the speaker says by believing her testimony. The theory that I propose maintains that a listener can come to know the truth of what a speaker says through an assumption of reliability, or through believing what the speaker says on the basis of reasons for doing so that she is aware of. It is just that, in such cases, the listener's knowledge is to be explained in terms other than transmission. The claim that the theory imposes overly restrictive conditions on knowledge from testimony is thus mistaken.

The theory that I propose can thus account for the two types of objection based on undefeated defeaters. The cases based on the incompatibility of transmission and SSI can, in fact, be accounted for in terms of the transmission of epistemic grounds. What is more, the characterisation of those cases motivated by SSI is compatible with the characterisation of them motivated by transmission. The objection based on cases in which it is altogether clearer that the speaker lacks epistemic grounds for what she says are to be accounted for differently. These, however, are no more problematic. In these cases, the claim that the listener comes to know what the speaker says depends on it being the case that the listener forms her belief in a way other than through an epistemic assumption, but the claim that the listener's knowledge is to be explained in terms of transmission depends on it being the case that the listener forms her belief through an epistemic assumption. The result is that the theory that I propose is equally not undermined by these cases.

7.4 Safety objections

A final type of counterexample has been developed against transmission theories. In these cases, the idea is that the listener's belief is safe in a way that the speaker's corresponding belief – and testimony – is not.[6] This type of case is developed by Sanford Goldberg (2005) and Charlie Pelling (2013). Unlike the creationist schoolteacher cases and the cases based on the incompatibility of SSI and transmission, the objections based on safety cannot be characterised in terms of the transmission of epistemic grounds. What is more, unlike the cases where the speaker has no epistemic grounds for what she says, the intuition that there is a difference in terms of safety is compatible with the stipulation that the listener forms her belief through an epistemic assumption. The result is that the counterexamples based on differences in safety present possibly the strongest line of objection to transmission theories, including the one I propose.

Goldberg's case involves someone who sees a milk carton in the refrigerator and forms the belief that there is milk in the refrigerator. She then tells a listener that this is the case. The speaker's belief is not safe because, at that time of day, there might easily have been an empty milk carton in the refrigerator and she would have nonetheless believed that there was milk in the refrigerator. Since the speaker says this because she believes it, her testimony is equally unsafe. There is, however, also an observer in the room who knows that there is milk in the refrigerator who would have intervened to stop the listener believing the speaker if she were to have said something false. The result is that, not easily would the listener have believed that there was milk in the refrigerator if this were not the case. The listener's belief is safe in a way that the speaker's belief is not (Goldberg 2005, p. 302).

In Pelling's case, a farmer hears a sound that could have been made by anything, but her paranoia leads her to think that a particular individual is trespassing on her land. As a result, she shouts that the individual is trespassing on her land. Her belief is the product of a paranoid hunch and is therefore unsafe, but her voice is such that it can only be heard by people on her land and her land extends much further than the range of her voice. The subject, however, is on her land. Although she is not the source of the noise the farmer heard, the individual hears the farmer when she shouts. Thus, the individual forms the belief that she is on the farmer's land. Her belief is safe in a way that the farmer's belief is not. For if she had not been on the farmer's land, she would not have heard the farmer shout and would not have formed the belief that she was on the farmer's land. On the other hand, the farmer would easily have believed that the individual was on her land if she had not been, since her belief is the product of a paranoid hunch (Pelling 2013, p. 213).

The argument that emerges from these cases is by now a familiar one:

(43)   The listener can come to know what the speaker says by believing her testimony.

(44)   If the listener's knowledge cannot be explained in terms of transmission, then transmission theories are false.

(45)   The listener's knowledge cannot be explained in terms of transmission.

Therefore

(46)   Transmission theories are false.

It is highly intuitive that the listener can come to know what the speaker says by believing her testimony in each case, as **(43)** states. The idea is that, in Goldberg's case, the observer's disposition to intervene means that the listener's belief has the modal profile required for knowing. In Pelling's case, the modal profile of the listener's belief is the product of the fact that the speaker's land extends much further than the range of her voice. Importantly, in both cases, the intuition that the listeners come to know in both cases does not subside with the stipulation that each listener forms her beliefs through an epistemic assumption about the speaker. The facts that determine the modal profile of their beliefs still seem to do so, even given the stipulation that the listeners form their beliefs through an epistemic assumption. On the face of it, this establishes both **(44)** and **(45)**.

Of course, those who doubt that the listener knowing is a matter of her belief having the right modal profile might be apt to resist the claim that the listener knows what she says. The transmission theories given by Burge (1993, 1997, 2013) and Faulkner (2011) do not accept that facts about the modal profile of the belief determine its status as knowledge. But the theory that I propose certainly does allow that knowing is a matter of belief with the appropriate modal profile, since it allows that knowledge from testimony can be grounded in the reliability of the processes involved in the production of the speaker's testimony or the reliability of the listener's comprehension processes. Even if denying **(43)** might, in principle, be an option for other transmission theories, it is not an option for the theory I propose.

These points notwithstanding, the counterexamples based on safety do not undermine the transmission theory that I propose. The key to seeing this is the observation from Chapter 1, in which I observed that the transmission of knowledge and epistemic grounds is, in certain ways, similar to the acquisition of a collection of ancient Roman coins. One way in which they are similar is that, in much the same way that you cannot acquire more ancient Roman coins from me than I have, I also cannot transmit epistemic grounds to you if I have none. Another similarity was the point that acquiring ancient Roman coins from me might bring you to have more ancient Roman coins than I had if you also acquired some from somewhere else. Something similar is true of the transmission of epistemic grounds, and it is this point that is important here.

In each case, it can be stipulated that the listener forms her belief through an epistemic assumption. This is a necessary condition of the speaker's epistemic grounds for what she says coming to be the listener's epistemic grounds for what the speaker says. But it does not entail that the speaker's epistemic grounds for what she says are the only epistemic grounds that can support the listener's belief in such a situation. In a case where a listener's belief is connected to the speaker's epistemic grounds for what she says, it does not follow that the listener's belief cannot also be supported by epistemic grounds from another source. Furthermore, the additional epistemic grounds acquired in this way account for the difference in safety between the speaker's belief and the listener's belief in each of the above cases. This idea is the key to seeing why the cases based on safety do not undermine the theory that I propose.

Consider again the case described by Goldberg. Exactly how we should characterise the case is unclear because it is unclear whether or not we should think that the speaker has epistemic grounds for thinking that there is milk in the refrigerator in virtue of the fact that she saw a milk carton there, or whether we should think that the speaker lacks epistemic grounds for what she says since there might easily have been an empty carton in the refrigerator at that time. Either way, the situation is unproblematic for the theory that I propose. If the speaker has epistemic grounds for what she says, then the epistemic grounds that underpin the listener's knowledge are the speaker's epistemic grounds in conjunction with those that come from the observer's disposition to intervene to prevent the listener forming a false belief. If the speaker does not have epistemic grounds for what she says, then the epistemic grounds that underpin the listener's knowledge come exclusively from the observer's disposition to intervene. In either case, the idea is that the listener's belief is connected to the speaker's epistemic grounds for what she says and also by the observer's disposition to intervene.

In the case described by Pelling, it is clear that the speaker does not have epistemic grounds for what she says. Her belief is just the product of a paranoid hunch, and she therefore has no epistemic grounds for thinking that the individual is on her land. The result is that the epistemic grounds that underpin the listener's knowledge come from the fact that the range of the speaker's voice is much shorter than the extent of her land. This, however, is compatible with the idea that, in virtue of the way that it is formed, the listener's belief is connected to the speaker's epistemic grounds in the way associated with transmission. The speaker's testimony does not make epistemic grounds available to transmit, because it is not epistemically sincere. There are two reasons for this. The first is that the speaker lacks epistemic grounds for what she says. The second is that, even if she did have epistemic grounds, these are not why she says that the listener is on her land. She says that the listener is on her land because of her paranoia. Hence, her testimony is epistemically insincere.

These cases illustrate the importance of the fact that a listener's belief being connected to the speaker's epistemic grounds for what she says does not entail that it is only the speaker's epistemic grounds that can underpin the listener's belief. But this is entirely compatible with the idea of transmission, and it is entirely compatible with the idea that transmission is indispensable to the epistemology of testimony. In other words, the theory allows for knowledge that is partially testimonial in character. The result, the fact that each listener believes what the speaker says through an epistemic assumption notwithstanding, is that the claim in **(44)** is false. The cases can be characterised in terms that are compatible with transmission, even if not in terms of transmission itself. The cases based on safety thus do not undermine the theory that I propose.

7.5 Conclusion

Arguments against transmission theories in the epistemology of testimony take various forms. Nonetheless, the theory that I propose is able to provide adequate characterisations of each of the cases presented against transmission theories. Furthermore, each of the lines of response uses principles that can be motivated independently of these cases. The principles needed to account for the cases presented against transmission theories can be motivated simply by the basic idea behind transmission and what it involves.

In order to account for the creationist schoolteacher cases and the cases that purport to establish the incompatibility of transmission and SSI, it is important that the transmission of epistemic grounds is the more fundamental notion of transmission. The cases can be characterised in terms of the transmission of epistemic grounds, though not the transmission of knowledge, and the result is that they can be characterised in terms of transmission in the most fundamental sense.

Accounting for the cases based on undefeated defeaters requires the observation that a listener's knowledge being explained in terms of transmission depends on her forming her belief through an epistemic assumption. If it is stipulated that the listener does this, then the theory that I propose yields a reason for thinking that the listener does not come to know what the speaker says. Furthermore, the theory that I propose can accommodate the intuition that the listener can come to know what the speaker says by allowing that her knowledge can be grounded in the reliability of the processes involved in the production of the speaker's testimony.

Lastly, the theory that I propose can account for cases in which there is a difference in terms of safety between a speaker's belief and the listener's corresponding belief. The acquisition of epistemic grounds through transmission is similar to the acquisition of a collection of ancient Roman coins in various ways. One of these is that someone might come to have more ancient Roman coins than someone else had by acquiring her collection; a listener might come to have better epistemic grounds than a speaker by acquiring the speaker's epistemic grounds for what she says. As a result, the observation that a listener's belief might be safe, where a speaker's corresponding belief is not, does not undermine transmission approaches to testimony.

Notes

1 J. Adam Carter and Philip J. Nickel (2014) develop the details of the case further, but the basic structure of the argument remains the same.
2 It also explains how to account for the version of the case that Carter and Nickel (2014) develop in which a scientist who does not believe the evolutionary proposition she discovers ultimately communicates it to the creationist schoolteacher. For a further discussion of this case, see Stephen Wright (2016).
3 On the exposition and defence of SSI, see also Jason Stanley (2005).
4 Cf. Faulkner (2011) seeks to accommodate this idea in terms of the listener's knowledge being grounded in the listener's reasons for believing the speaker's testimony that the listener is aware of.
5 I have suggested this line of response in Stephen Wright (2015).
6 Whilst the cases are developed in terms of safety, they can equally be modified to generate differences in terms of reliability or sensitivity.

Bibliography

Audi, R. (2006). Testimony, credulity, and veracity. In J. Lackey and E. Sosa (Eds.), *The Epistemology of Testimony*, pp. 25–49. Oxford: Oxford University Press.

Burge, T. (1993). Content preservation. *Philosophical Review* 102(4), 457–488.

Burge, T. (1997). Interlocution, perception, and memory. *Philosophical Studies* 86(1), 21–47.

Burge, T. (2013). Postscript: Content preservation. In T. Burge (Ed.), *Cognition Through Understanding: Self-Knowledge, Interlocution, Reasoning, Reflection: Philosophical Essays Volume 3*. Oxford: Oxford University Press.

Carter, J. A. and P. J. Nickel (2014). On testimony and transmission. *Episteme* 11(2), 145–155.

Faulkner, P. (2011). *Knowledge on Trust*. Oxford: Oxford University Press.

Goldberg, S. (2005). Testimonial knowledge through unsafe testimony. *Analysis* 65(288), 302–311.

Graham, P. (2006). Can testimony generate knowledge? *Philosophica* 78, 105–127.

Hawthorne, J. (2004). *Knowledge and Lotteries*. Oxford: Oxford University Press.

Lackey, J. (2008). *Learning from Words: Testimony as a Source of Knowledge*. Oxford: Oxford University Press.

MacFarlane, J. (2005). Knowledge laundering: Testimony and sensitive invariant-ism. *Analysis* 65(2), 132–138.

Pelling, C. (2013). Testimony, testimonial belief, and safety. *Philosophical Studies* 164(1), 205–217.

Stanley, J. (2005). *Knowledge and Practical Interests*. Oxford: Oxford University Press.

Wright, S. (2015). In defence of transmission. *Episteme* 12(1), 13–28.

Wright, S. (2016). The transmission of knowledge and justification. *Synthese* 193(1), 293–311.

Index

110   *Index*

For Product Safety Concerns and Information please contact our EU representative GPSR@taylorandfrancis.com Taylor & Francis Verlag GmbH, Kaufingerstraße 24, 80331 München, Germany

Printed and bound by CPI Group (UK) Ltd, Croydon, CR0 4YY

11/04/2025

01844008-0005